ORTHO'S All About
Orchids

Meredith® Books
Des Moines, Iowa

Ortho® Books
An imprint of Meredith® Books

All About Orchids
Principal Garden Writer: Elvin McDonald
Editor: Marilyn Rogers
Contributing Editors: Leona H. Openshaw, Kate Jerome
Contributing Technical Editor: Ned Nash
Art Director: Tom Wegner
Copy Chief: Catherine Hamrick
Copy and Production Editor: Terri Fredrickson
Contributing Copy Editor: James A. Baggett
Contributing Proofreaders: Kathy Roth Eastman,
    Raymond Kast
Contributing Prop/Photo Stylists: Peggy Johnston
Indexer: Don Glassman
Electronic Production Coordinator: Paula Forest
Editorial and Design Assistants: Kathleen Stevens,
    Karen Schirm
Production Director: Douglas M. Johnston
Production Manager: Pam Kvitne
Assistant Prepress Manager: Marjorie J. Schenkelberg

Additional Editorial Contributions from
    Art Rep Services
Director: Chip Nadeau
Designer: lk Design
Illustrator: Vera Wong

Meredith® Books
Editor in Chief: James D. Blume
Design Director: Matt Strelecki
Managing Editor: Gregory H. Kayko
Executive Ortho Editor: Benjamin W. Allen

Director, Sales & Marketing, Retail: Michael A. Peterson
Director, Sales & Marketing, Special Markets:
    Rita McMullen
Director, Sales & Marketing, Home & Garden Center
    Channel: Ray Wolf
Director, Operations: George A. Susral

Vice President, General Manager: Jamie L. Martin

Meredith Publishing Group
President, Publishing Group: Christopher M. Little
Vice President, Consumer Marketing & Development:
    Hal Oringer

Meredith Corporation
Chairman and Chief Executive Officer: William T. Kerr
Chairman of the Executive Committee: E.T. Meredith III

Cover photograph: Phalaenopsis by Lynn Harrison

All of us at Ortho® Books are dedicated to providing you
with the information and ideas you need to enhance your
home and garden. We welcome your comments and
suggestions about this book. Write to us at:
    Meredith Corporation
    Ortho Books
    1716 Locust St.
    Des Moines, IA 50309-3023

If you would like more information on other Ortho
products, call 800-225-2883 or visit us at www.ortho.com

Special thanks to Ned Nash and the American Orchid
Society for their invaluable assistance and technical
expertise.

Thanks to
Iowa Orchids and Dr. Robert Bannister, Janet Anderson,
Aimee Reiman, Melissa George, Mary Irene Swartz

Photographers
(Photographers credited may retain copyright ©
    to the listed photographs.)
L= Left, R= Right, C= Center, B= Bottom, T= Top
William D. Adams: p. 4, (TL), 30 (B), 45 (BR, lower inset),
    58 (BC, BR);
Greg Allikas: p. 3, (C, B), 7 (B), 19 (C), 20 (L), 21 (R),
    22 (L), 23, 33 (C), 35, 36 (L, TR), 43 (TL, BL),
    44 (BL/large), 50, 52, 56–57, 58 (TR, BL), 60 (BL, BC),
    62 (TR), 64 (TR), 68 (TR), 75, 78 (TR, BL, BR), 79,
    80 (TR), 91;
Patricia Bruno/Positive Images: p. 15;
Scott Camazine: p. 44 (BL inset), 47 (BR), 66 (BL);
Barbara J. Coxe: p. 36 (BR);
Charles Marden Fitch: p. 33 (T), 44 (BL/small, BR),
    45 (CL, BR/small), 47 (L) 71 (BR), 78 (BC), 89 (B),
    90 (BC);
Dennis Frates/Positive Images: p. 55;
John Glover: p. 3 (T), 4–5, 19 (B), 62 (BL), 64 (BL, BC),
    65, 66 (TR), 70 (TR), 74 (BC), 76 (BL), 77, 81, 86,
    88 (B);
Jerry Harpur: p. 54 (BL), 59, 66 (BC, BR), 80 (BC), 82,
    90 (BL);
Marcus Harpur: p. 72 (BL);
Stephen Ingram: p. 76 (TR);
judywhite/New Leaf Images: p. 42, 44 (BR inset), 45 (TL),
    46 (B), 47 (TR), 72 (TR), 89 (T);
Dency Kane: p. 80 (BR), 84 (BL);
Andrew Lawson: p. 67, 68 (BL), 73;
Allan Mandell: p. 62 (BC);
David McDonald/PhotoGarden: p. 60 (BR), 62 (BR),
    74 (BR), 80 (BL), 85;
Elvin McDonald: p. 74 (TR), 83, 87 (T);
Steven McDonald: p. 20 (R), 21 (L), 25 (R), 40 (BC),
    41 (B);
Clive Nichols: p. 7 (C), 64 (BR);
Susan A. Roth: p. 19 (T), 74 (BL), 87 (B);
Kevin Schafer: p. 61, 72 (BC, BR), 76 (BR);
Richard Shiell: p. 4 (BL), 7 (T), 22 (R), 43 (TR, CR, BR),
    44 (T), 45 (TR, BR/large), 47 (RC), 54 (T, BR), 63,
    76 (BC), 84 (TR), 88 (T);
Pam Spaulding/Positive Images: p. 34 (R), 71 (TL);
Steve Struse: p. 8, 9, 10, 11, 12 (R), 13, 14, 24, 25 (L), 26,
    27, 28, 29, 30 (L), 31, 32, 33 (B), 37, 38, 39, 40 (all but
    BC), 41 (T), 48, 49, 53;
Michael S. Thompson: p. 60 (TR), 69, 70 (BL), 90 (BR).

ORCHID PRIMER 4

BUYING, GROWING, AND CARING FOR ORCHIDS 18

ORCHID PROBLEMS 42

ORCHID BOTANY AND NOMENCLATURE 48

ORCHID GALLERY 56

ORCHID PRIMER

In nature, orchids grow primarily in trees as epiphytes (air plants) or in the ground as terrestrials (earth plants). Those from the trees tend to make the best houseplants, but because they are epiphytic, their needs for light, water, humidity, growing medium, and fertilizer can be different in some ways from ordinary houseplants. However, "different" isn't necessarily synonymous with difficult.

Any reputation orchids may have for being finicky stems from a fundamental misunderstanding about their origins. When the word "jungle" is used, one thinks immediately of hot, dank, steamy, and even dark conditions. Jungle is a misnomer in this context, for literally a jungle is an early stage of what eventually becomes a "rain forest," a noun coined in 1903 to define "a tropical woodland with an annual rainfall of at least 100 inches and marked by lofty broad-leaved evergreen trees forming a continuous canopy."

It is in this lofty canopy where most of the epiphytic orchids originate, up in the air where moist breezes blow and there is abundant sunlight. But orchids of one kind or another grow almost all over the world. Species endemic to higher elevations may be accustomed to cool night temperatures while those near sea level may be adapted to more heat around the clock.

Success with orchids is this simple: Identify the existing conditions in your home, or conditions that are easy to modify, then select orchids that nature has outfitted to like—even love—living in these conditions. Further, invest regularly in flowering orchids, and you will build a collection that blooms in all seasons.

Phalaenopsis orchids (large photo) are native to climates with even amounts of moisture year-round. Laelia crispata (inset, below) prefers distinct wet and dry seasons. Many hybrids, such as 'Bandolino' (inset, top), are often more adaptable to varying conditions than their parents.

ORCHID ENVIRONMENTS: LIGHT

When they are in bloom, orchid flowers will last longer if they are in bright light but protected from hot sun shining directly on them. Stronger rays are needed for regeneration.

The first step in growing orchids is to take a close look at the available conditions. How much light is there? What is the temperature range? These factors are the ones you will most likely want to consider at first, because they are the most difficult and expensive to modify. Other factors, such as humidity and ventilation, can be altered easily. (The amount of light, heat, water, and air that orchids require is described in the following section. Use this information to help you determine the type of orchid environment you can most readily provide.)

BRIGHT LIGHT

Like most other flowering plants, orchids often grow and bloom best in as much light as they can tolerate without burning. Thus, if there are several spots in your home where you might want to grow orchids, the brightest is nearly always the best. An unobstructed south-facing window is ideal because it receives bright light for most of the day and will usually capture enough light to carry the plants through the winter. However, you need to be careful in summer; a south-facing window can burn even the most light-demanding species. A number of orchids will

thrive in east- or west-facing windows, but keep in mind that the duration of light is as important as brightness—two hours of searing afternoon sunlight are no substitute for six hours of diffuse radiance. Plants can use only so much light energy; any extra stresses them.

The direction a window faces gives only a general indication of how much light is available to the plants inside. Many windows are shaded by outdoor plants or roof overhangs, and outdoor light levels vary from region to region. Also, the color and texture of walls and other surfaces inside the window influence the intensity of light in the room. For these reasons, many growers shy away from imprecise descriptions of exposure and discuss light in terms of a standard measurement, the footcandle.

LIGHT REQUIREMENTS: Measure the light intensity in your growing area (see "Using a Camera to Measure Light Intensity" and "Measuring Light with Hand Shadows," page 8), then you can choose the kinds of orchids that will grow best for you. The chart at right shows the light requirements of the orchids described in this book. Notice that most of them adapt to light intensities in the medium range—1,500 to 3,000 footcandles. Some species within a genus—or some of their

IDEAL LIGHT RANGES IN FOOTCANDLES

PLANT NAME	LIGHT RANGE							
	Low			Medium			High	
	500	1,000	1,500	2,000	2,500	3,000	3,500	4,000 footcandles
Brassavola				███	███	███	███	
Brassia				███	███	███		
Cattleya				███	███	███	███	
Cymbidium								
standard				███	███	███	███	
miniature			███	███	███	███		
Dendrobium			███	███	███	███	███	███
Epidendrum			███	███	███	███	███	███
Laelia			███	███	███	███	███	███
Ludisia		███	███					
Masdevallia	███	███	███	███				
Miltonia	███	███	███	███				
Odontoglossum		███	███	███	███	███	███	███
Oncidium				███	███	███	███	
Paphiopedilum								
green-leaf				███	███			
mottled-leaf			███	███				
Phalaenopsis		███	███					
Phragmipedium					███	███	███	
Sophronitis			███	███	███			
Vanda					███	███	███	███

Sunburned leaf: too much light

Adequate light: Plenty of blooms

The orchid on the left has received ample light. It will produce many blossoms. The dark green leaves of the one on the right indicate it has received too little light. It's doubtful that it will bloom.

hybrids—may be exceptions. An intergeneric hybrid (a cross of plants in two or more genera) may tolerate a broader range of light intensities than either parent. Before purchasing an unfamiliar orchid, find out as much as you can about its light requirements.

If you already have some orchids, the most practical way to see if they are receiving the right amount of light is to look at the plants themselves. When orchids are receiving the right amount of light, their leaves are light to medium green and the pseudobulbs are full and firm. The plants also bloom dependably, if other conditions are right.

With too little light, leaves are unable to manufacture enough food for the plant to grow and bloom well. Leaves are elongated, flimsy, and dark green. Pseudobulbs are soft or shriveled. And the flowers—if they appear at all—are undersized, faded, and floppy.

At the other extreme, orchids that get too much light are often scorched. The leaves may have a yellow or reddish tinge. Although the plant may bloom, the flower buds and racemes may be deformed and the edges of the petals browned—a result of water stress.

Direct sun can burn orchids during the brightest hours from late winter to fall in most regions, and year-round in southern areas and at high elevations. Generally, plants with thick leathery leaves are slow to burn; plants with thin leaves burn easily. However, phalaenopsis leaves, which may seem thick and leathery, are ill equipped to take full sun and burn quickly as do those of paphiopedilums. Cymbidiums, cattleyas, dendrobiums, and oncidiums have foliage that if gradually conditioned will take large doses of sun in much the same way some human skin tans beautifully rather than burns.

Besides intensity of light, there is also the matter of duration, usually referred to as day length. Some orchids bloom as the days grow longer, as spring moves toward summer; others are the opposite, blooming as the days shorten, as fall dwindles into early winter. For these, flowering may be prevented by any exposure to light beyond a 12-hour day at the time they are preparing to bloom.

Another consideration is spectrum of color in the light. Orchids use reds and blues but not greens, which they reflect. Red is critical for flowering. If growing under lights, a 50-50 combination of cool-white and warm-white tubes provides the essential balance of red and blue rays for healthy plants.

ORCHID ENVIRONMENTS: LIGHT
continued

The most accurate way to make sure that plants are receiving enough light is to measure the light intensity with a footcandle light meter. Different meters are available. Some come equipped with a separate sensor to allow you to easily read the dial while measuring the light from different angles. Other, one-piece meters have the sensor built into the top of the unit.

USING A CAMERA TO MEASURE LIGHT INTENSITY

Any camera with a built-in light meter will provide fairly accurate readings that can be translated into footcandles. Set the film speed at ASA 25 and the shutter speed at ¹⁄₆₀th of a second. Aim the camera at a flat sheet of matte, white paper or cardboard, held at the level where the plant's leaves would be. Hold the camera close enough so that all you see when you look through the viewfinder is the paper. Be sure not to block the light with your head, hands, or camera. Adjust the f-stop (lens opening) until a correct exposure for taking a picture is shown on the light meter in the camera. Use the table below to convert the f-stop setting into a footcandle estimate.

For best results, take the readings at the brightest time of a sunny day, preferably in summer. This will give you an idea of the maximum intensity to which the plants will be exposed and will enable you to avoid scorching them with too much light. The average light intensity (of long-term importance to growth and flowering) is harder to measure accurately, but you can estimate it by taking several readings at different times over a period of several days–weekends or holidays when you can stay home.

F-stop	Footcandles
f/2.8	200
f/4	370
f/5.6	750
f/8	1,500
f/11	2,800
f/16	5,000

MEASURING LIGHT IN FOOTCANDLES

A footcandle is the amount of light falling on a 1-square-foot surface located 1 foot away from one candle. Unless you do your evening reading as Abraham Lincoln did, this probably doesn't mean much to you.

Here are some more familiar examples: The light intensity outdoors at noon on a clear summer day may be as high as 10,000 footcandles; a midday reading on an overcast winter day may be as low as 500 footcandles. As you would expect, the intensity of light indoors is much lower. The direct sunlight entering a window on a clear summer day may be as high as 8,000 footcandles next to the glass, but is usually closer to 4,000 to 5,000 footcandles. At the same time, the intensity of light in the shade at the side of a very bright window may be only 600 footcandles. The brightness of electric lights can be deceiving. A supermarket seems very bright, but the light intensity is usually only

MEASURING LIGHT WITH HAND SHADOWS

In the same direct way that using your fingers can tell you instantly about moisture conditions in a pot of growing medium, so too can using your hand tell you about the degree of light reaching the leaves of an orchid plant. Position yourself so that you can hold your hand about a foot from the plant, between it and the window. If you can see no shadow at all, there may not be enough light to grow any orchid, only to enjoy it while in bloom. A possible exception is the jewel orchid, *Ludisia* var. *discolor dawsoniana*, which is grown primarily for its

beautiful leaves and tends to thrive in less light rather than more. If you see a faint to moderate shadow, there is probably adequate light for phalaenopsis and paphiopedilums.

If you see a sharp shadow, this indicates sufficiently bright light to grow ascocenda, cattleya, cymbidium, dendrobium, epidendrum, encyclia, laelia, oncidium, and many other orchids.

about 500 footcandles. Because our pupils adjust so effectively to light, we can't really estimate light intensity merely by looking. The easiest and most accurate way to learn how much light is available to the plants is to measure it with a footcandle light meter (see "Orchid Resources," page 92). Be sure to purchase a meter that can measure light intensities at least as high as 5,000 footcandles. The most commonly used meter, made by General Electric, has a filter that clips over the sensor for use at high-light intensities.

If you don't want to purchase a light meter that specifically measures light in footcandles, you can estimate light intensity using a photographic meter or a camera with a built-in light meter. Most cameras have light meters that measure light intensity in f-stops. See "Using a Camera to Measure Light Intensity" on page 8 for simple instructions on converting f-stops into footcandles.

MODIFYING LIGHT

Diffusing midday sunlight, making some shade, or otherwise reducing the intensity of sunlight on your orchids poses no problem. Easily opened sheer or open-weave curtains may be all you need. Vertical blinds are ideal because they can be adjusted to allow the right amount of light to fall on plants. The moving bars of sunlight shining through the slats of a vertical blind mimic the play of dappled light through the leaves of trees. Horizontal blinds are not as efficient in modifying light because the sun tends to move across the plants in the same band, which can over-expose some parts while shading the rest of the plant.

You may not need to cover the windows with anything if you can move the plants back a few feet; light intensity decreases rapidly as you move away from the source.

GROWING ORCHIDS UNDER LIGHTS

Some of the finest orchids grow and bloom where there is little or no sunlight. Electric lights will brighten a marginally sunny windowsill, illuminate a bookshelf growing area, or transform a windowless basement into a tropical wonderland. Growing orchids under lights is similar to growing them on a windowsill—their requirements for light, humidity, water, and fertilizer are the same. In this case, though, you adjust the amount of light the plant receives by adjusting its distance from the lights and by varying the length of time the lights are on.

In some ways, electric lights are better than sunlight for orchids. Grown in the sun, few

LIGHT TIPS

Light is a key ingredient in successful orchid growing. Too much light will burn the leaves, too little light—or light at the wrong time—will keep the plants from flowering. Follow these tips to make sure your plants are receiving the illumination they need to grow and bloom.

■ Turn plants occasionally to keep them from becoming lopsided. Don't turn them when they are in bud, though, or the flowers may twist around at awkward angles to face the sun.
■ Move an underexposed orchid into stronger light one step at a time over a period of several weeks. If you are using a light meter, try to increase the light intensity by no more than 100 to 200 footcandles at a time.
■ Remove plants from full sun once their flowers have opened. Bright sunlight can make the colors fade.
■ Watch new acquisitions closely to be sure they don't burn before they adapt to a possibly stronger exposure than that to which they were accustomed.
■ If you suspect a plant is receiving too much sun, feel the leaves. If to the touch of your fingers they feel noticeably warmer than the surrounding air, reduce the light intensity.
■ Be sure to keep your plants and windows clean—dust and dirt block valuable sunlight and rob your indoor garden of sustenance.
■ Some orchids need a period of uninterrupted darkness at night in order to flower. Plants growing in a living area may be prevented from flowering by the illumination of a single table lamp. The "Orchid Gallery," beginning on page 56, notes whether an orchid is light sensitive.

plants have unblemished leaves; grown under lights, plants can have perfect foliage. The cool glow of the lights can't burn the leaves, and the plants grow more symmetrically because the light comes from directly overhead. Also, the constant intensity of the lights ensures that the leaves will all be approximately the same size no matter what time of year they are produced.

MAXIMIZING LIGHT INTENSITY: Do everything you can to maximize the light intensity for your plants—you can't overexpose them to fluorescent light. Use fixtures with reflectors. Paint the walls and other surfaces in the growing area with flat white paint. To flower well, orchids need to be placed close to the tubes, with the tops of the leaves 3 to 6 inches beneath. Most commercially available plant stands have adjustable shelves. If you build your own light garden, suspend the fixtures over the plants with chains so that you can adjust the distance link by link. Place small plants on inverted

ORCHID ENVIRONMENTS: LIGHT
continued

pots to bring their leaves up to an adequate level like those of the larger, taller specimens. **CHOOSING THE RIGHT SPOT:** You probably have several places in your home suitable for growing orchids under lights. If your garden is near a window, you may not need as many lights and the plants will respond well to the natural light. By using a basement, stairwell, or any other out-of-the-way place, you can create a growing area without sacrificing needed living space. The concrete floors and walls of most basements normally are unharmed by humidity or a little water. Some growers line the walls and ceilings of their basement growing areas with plastic to maintain the humidity. If the basement or space has no windows, a fan or two will take care of the plants' needs for air movement.

Ready-made light gardens for orchids are available. Multi-tiered stands and carts with built-in humidity trays and fluorescent lights are offered in a variety of sizes and provide an easy solution to a lack of light. Simple units consisting of a fixture and frame are designed to light a small table or shelf.

If you are a do-it-yourselfer, you will find it simple to build your own light garden with the components offered by lighting supply stores and mail-order suppliers. See "Orchid Resources," page 92, for companies that specialize in indoor gardening equipment. **TYPES OF LIGHTS:** Fluorescent lights—the tubes used in offices and classrooms—turn electricity into light more efficiently than do the incandescent lights used in homes.

■ FLUORESCENT LIGHTS: Full-spectrum bulbs emit light with a spectral distribution approaching that of sunlight. These bulbs give a more natural rendering of plant colors while producing the wavelengths required for growth and flowering. Trade names include Tru-Bloom®, Naturescent®, Gro-Lux WS®, and Vita-Lite®. Standard "cool" white and "warm" white fluorescents are much less expensive and, if used in a 50:50 ratio, provide a satisfactory balance of light rays for vigorous growth and flowering.

■ FLUORESCENT FIXTURES: The best fixtures for orchid growing are 48 or 96 inches long, hold four 40-watt or 74-watt bulbs, and are made of aluminum. Aluminum fixtures resist corrosion and conduct heat away from

Orchid plants in bloom look especially beautiful when placed within the circle of brightest light cast by a desk or floor lamp. Be sure the flowers are not close enough to the light bulb to actually be warmed by it, because if they are, the heat will quickly age them.

the lighting unit most effectively. A fixture that is going to be the plant's only source of light should hold four bulbs. Two-bulb fixtures will suffice for supplementing natural light, or they can be paired to simulate a four-bulb fixture. Four 40-watt tubes in a 48-inch fixture will adequately light a growing space 2 by 4 feet; four 74-watt tubes in a 96-inch fixture will light a plant bench 3 by 8 feet.

In addition to holding the tubes, the fixture houses a ballast, a transformer that regulates the power. Ballasts vary in quality; the better they are, the less power they use, the less heat they produce, and the longer they last. Electronic ballasts are the coolest and most efficient, also the most expensive.

■ OTHER KINDS OF LIGHTS: Mercury vapor, high-pressure sodium, and quartz lamps are much brighter than fluorescent lamps, but they are also much more expensive to

LIGHTING SYSTEM PROS AND CONS

■ Incandescent light bulbs burn too hot to be placed in close proximity to orchid plants. Sockets for one or two are sometimes configured into a fluorescent fixture; there, 25- or 40-watt bulbs may be burned as a way of gaining sufficient red rays to boost flowering. Any part of the orchid plant that touches an incandescent bulb will burn.

■ Table and floor lamps outfitted with incandescent bulbs can be an ideal source for illuminating an orchid plant in bloom, provided the flowers are at least 12 to 18 inches from the light bulbs.

■ Reflector floodlights and spotlights, which have built-in reflectors, in 75-watt strength can be used in a ceramic socket and placed 3 feet or more from flowering orchids to show them off, adding drama and emphasizing color, shape, form, and texture.

■ The heat given off by all types of incandescents has a drying effect in the immediate vicinity, which can be offset by setting the orchid plants on a pebble humidity tray or by operating a cool-vapor humidifier in the same room.

■ Fluorescent lights are more efficient than incandescents and give off relatively little heat. It is best to keep orchid plant parts from actually touching the tubes, however, otherwise they may be disfigured.

■ Fluorescent fixtures have a utilitarian appearance at best. They can be hidden behind a valance or used in a room where the way they look doesn't matter.

purchase and maintain. Their chief advantage is brightness—a quartz lamp will sustain orchids with light needs that can't be met with fluorescents. Because they are so bright (and hot) they are placed farther from the plants and can thus illuminate tall plants that would not fit under fluorescent fixtures. These lights require special fixtures that must be installed by an electrician.

ADJUSTING DAY LENGTH: What fluorescent lights lack in intensity, they can make up in duration. Use a timer to set the day length for your plants. Some orchids require seasonal variations in day length in order to bloom. For these, you will need to adjust the timer every few months to mimic the seasons, as follows:

November to January	16 hours/day
February to June	18 hours/day
July to August	16 hours/day
September to October	12 hours/day

This schedule keeps the temperature in the growing area tolerable during the hottest part of the year, and brings spring-flowering plants into bloom for the holidays.

ORCHIDS UNDER LIGHTS

Almost any orchid can be grown under lights, but the most successful are compact plants that fit readily under the tubes so that most of their foliage is bathed in bright light. Tall, light-loving plants such as vandas and the tall dendrobiums won't fit. But plants such as the phalaenopsis, with short foliage and long flower spikes, grow well under lights if you train the spikes between and around the fixtures as they are developing. To get started, try any of these orchids in your first light garden:

Cattleya (compact hybrids best)
Dendrobium (compact species such as
    D. kingianum and D. cuthbertsonii)
Encyclia cochleata
Encyclia tampensis
Ludisia discolor
Macodes petola
Masdevallia (if conditions are cool enough)
Miltonia (species and hybrids)
Odontoglossum (multigeneric hybrids)
Oncidium (small species and hybrids)
Paphiopedilum (excellent for beginners)
Phalaenopsis (practically foolproof)
Phragmipedium
Sophronitis

When growing orchids in living areas, keep in mind that some species require a night of uninterrupted darkness for flowering. These light-sensitive species include unifoliate (single-leaved) cattleyas such as *Cattleya labiata, C. mossiae, C. percivaliana,* and *C. trianae.* Other orchids sensitive to night lighting include *Bulbophyllum falcatum, Dendrobium phalaenopsis, Oncidium splendidum,* and *Phalaenopsis amabilis.* A reading lamp left on at night produces enough light to keep these plants from blooming.

Aside from occasionally wiping the dust off the tubes, all you have to do to keep your lights burning brightly is replace the tubes after they have been in service about a year.

Miniature, small, and compact hybrids of normally larger orchids are ideally suited to growing in a fluorescent-light garden equipped with at least four 40-watt tubes in a reflector.

SIMPLE LIGHT GARDENS

■ The smallest light garden that can be built to any worthwhile purpose is to install a reflector 24 inches long with two 20-watt fluorescent tubes over a 12- by 24-inch shelf. Suspend it so that the tubes are 12 to 15 inches above the shelf surface. Small orchid plants with beautiful foliage such as *Ludisia discolor* and *Macodes petola* can be accommodated in such a space, perhaps along with miniature gloxinias, African violets, begonias, and earth-star bromeliad *(Cryptanthus).*
■ To really grow some orchids under lights, install four 40-watt tubes equidistant in one or two reflectors 18 inches above a table or plant bench measuring 2 feet by 4 feet.
■ Even better is to install four 74-watt tubes equidistant in one or more reflectors 18 to 24 inches above a table or plant bench measuring 3 feet by 8 feet. This provides 24 square feet of growing space, equal in size to a bench in a home greenhouse. This configuration can be stacked so that it is a double-decker (48 square feet of growing space) or triple-decker (72 square feet of growing space) while using only 24 square feet of floor space.

ORCHID ENVIRONMENTS: TEMPERATURE

In nature, the temperature begins to drop when the sun sets and is at its lowest before dawn. Orchids are accustomed to this temperature fluctuation and, in fact, most of them depend on it. Without a day-night fluctuation of 10° to 15° F, the plants will grow plenty of healthy foliage but may stubbornly refuse to flower. Cool nighttime temperatures allow them to store rather than expend the carbohydrates they manufacture during the day—the carbohydrates they need to produce beautiful blossoms.

To make it easier to describe the temperature needs of orchids, orchid growers divide the plants into three temperature categories: warm, intermediate, and cool. Although the exact temperature ranges associated with these terms vary (some growers use wider ranges), the following ranges are most common:

WARM
80° to 90° F day
65° to 70° F night

INTERMEDIATE
70° to 80° F day
55° to 65° F night

COOL
60° to 70° F day
50° to 55° F night

Most orchids, like most people, prefer temperatures in the intermediate range. Given adequate humidity and ventilation, many orchids will tolerate higher daytime temperatures than those shown above—as long as they cool off at night. Thus, the night temperature is the most important temperature factor to consider when selecting orchids. Although some determined hobbyists have used space heaters, infrared lights, and heating cables to create a warm spot in their homes for orchids, such efforts are only necessary if you are trying to grow plants that require much warmer temperatures than you can naturally provide. It is much more practical to find out what temperatures you have and select the plants accordingly.

MEASURING TEMPERATURE

Unless you spend a great deal of time at home during the day and get up before dawn each morning, you may find you don't really know the maximum and minimum temperatures in your orchid-growing area. A special kind of thermometer, appropriately called a

A maximum-minimum thermometer helps take the guesswork out of finding the perfect spot for each orchid you wish to grow. Move it around and note the different ranges.

maximum-minimum thermometer, can measure these temperatures for you. A maximum-minimum thermometer generally has two sides; one side records the high temperature, and the other records the low. It also displays the current temperature. Mount the thermometer as close to the plants as possible, but keep it out of direct sunlight. Orchid-supply companies offer maximum-minimum thermometers (see "Orchid Resources" on page 92). They are moderately priced and are a wise investment.

TEMPERATURE TIPS

Temperatures can vary considerably within a given growing area.
■ At night, the temperature is coolest next to the windows and near the floor. During the day, especially in fair weather, the air next to the glass is the warmest air in the room. You can take advantage of these small-scale variations in temperature or eliminate them by mixing the air with a fan. When in doubt, place a maximum-minimum thermometer in the area so you will know precisely what temperatures your plants are experiencing within a 24-hour period.
■ Place orchids with lower temperature needs closer to the floor and those with higher temperature needs on shelves above them. Those on the top shelf will likely experience the highest temperatures.
■ Hang plastic curtains around windows to create microclimates that are cooler at night and warmer during the day.
■ Don't let plants touch the windows in the winter in cold regions.
■ Use a fan to circulate warm air or bring cool air in from another part of the house.
■ Be on the alert for any hot or cold drafts that may blow directly on your orchids.

ADDING BOTTOM HEAT

Sometimes as fate would have it, the only suitable lighting situation for orchids will be where temperatures are too cold in winter. For example, you may have an east-facing window with ideal light for phalaenopsis but for one reason or another that room is too chilly to suit them. A simple solution would be to build a wood flat sized to fit the top of your plant table and about 5 inches deep.

Line the flat with heavy plastic to prevent leaks. Pour about 3 inches of potting soil into the flat and level the surface. Place a soil-heating cable over the soil, cover it with another inch or so of soil, then top it off with a layer of gravel. Now place the orchid pots on the gravel and turn on the heating cable. Gentle bottom heat will help keep the orchids healthy even though air temperatures may be cooler than might be considered ideal.

Especially in older homes and apartments, radiators may be directly under the windows where you want to grow orchids. This situation can be turned to an advantage by hanging a shelf over the radiator or placing a table that is taller than the heating unit over it. Then outfit the surface with one or more pebble humidity trays. The more the heating unit is used, the more water will be evaporated from the trays into the air surrounding the orchids, thus giving them both gentle bottom heat and a pleasantly moist microclimate.

TEMPERATURE REQUIREMENTS

The chart at right shows the ideal night temperature ranges for the kinds of orchids in this book. You will notice that many kinds will grow in more than one temperature category. This may be a reflection of the orchid's adaptability, or it may be a result of plant breeding; many hybrids are much more adaptable than their parents. For example, a hybrid produced by crossing a cool-growing parent with an intermediate-growing parent may grow well in either temperature range.

MODIFYING TEMPERATURE

Many people customarily turn their thermostats down at night to 55° or 60° F to conserve energy. In addition to reducing the heating bill, this practice also satisfies the cool-night requirements of orchids. In a well-insulated house, however, the temperature may not drop enough. If this is the case, consider opening a window to allow the evening breezes to cool the plants. Ideally, an "orchid room" can be separated at night from the rest of the house by a closed door. The temperature in that room can then be allowed to drop without chilling the rest of the home.

Be sensitive to any hot or cold drafts blowing directly on your orchids, from heating and cooling units or from open windows and doors. Also be on the watch for microclimates, potential small growing spaces where temperatures are cooler or warmer than those elsewhere within the same room or space. Use a maximum-minimum thermometer to take out the guesswork.

IDEAL NIGHT TEMPERATURE RANGES

Plant name	Cool 50°–55° F	Intermediate 55–65° F	Warm 65°–70° F
Brassavola		███	███
Brassia	███	███	
Cattleya		███	
Cymbidium			
standard	███		
miniature	███	███	
Dendrobium	███	███	███
Epidendrum	███	███	███
Laelia		███	███
Ludisia		███	███
Masdevallia	███	███	
Miltonia	███	███	
Odontoglossum	███		
Oncidium		███	███
Paphiopedilum			
green-leaf	███	███	
mottled-leaf		███	███
Phalaenopsis		███	███
Phragmipedium	███	███	
Sophronitis	███	███	
Vanda		███	███

ORCHID ENVIRONMENTS: HUMIDITY AND AIR CIRCULATION

Most orchids grow best in a relative daytime humidity of about 40 to 70 percent. Humidity is moisture in the air, not water on the plants or in the growing medium. Airborne moisture keeps the plants from drying out in bright light and warm air, without encouraging the fungi and bacteria that can infect wet plants.

MEASURING HUMIDITY

An experienced orchid grower can tell whether the humidity is right by sniffing the air—or so some claim.

Hygrometers (instruments that measure humidity) are usually more reliable. The simplest and least-expensive hygrometers have a dial that shows the percentage of relative humidity. A fibrous material (the old ones used a hair) connected to the needle shrinks and swells depending on the humidity. More accurate (and more expensive) hygrometers are a combination of two thermometers. One of the thermometers measures the wet bulb temperature, the temperature of evaporating water; the other measures the dry bulb, or air temperature. By consulting a table, you can convert these temperatures to relative humidity. For most hobbyists, the inexpensive dial-type hygrometer is sufficient. Many orchid supply companies carry hygrometers. See "Orchid Resources" on page 92 for names and addresses.

RAISING HUMIDITY

Relative humidity falls as the temperature rises. To keep plants from drying out, you reverse this process. The simplest way to raise the humidity around plants is to grow them on water-filled trays or saucers filled with water and pebbles. Choose trays that are 100 percent watertight; plastic and fiberglass are

HUMIDITY TIPS

There are many ways to increase the humidity in a growing area. Here are some pointers for care of evaporation trays and some ideas for maintaining the moisture in the air around your plants.

■ Remove the pebbles from your evaporation tray every two or three months and wash them in a weak bleach solution to remove accumulated salts and algae. Do not add bleach or algaecide to water in the trays when they are in use.

■ Use a turkey baster to remove any excess water from the evaporation trays after you water your plants.

■ Mist your plants only if they will have plenty of time to dry off before nightfall.

■ Plants themselves are effective humidifiers. Group your plants to create an attractive display and humid microclimate, but don't place them so close that they restrict air circulation.

the most reliable. The tray should be a minimum of 1½ inches deep, filled to the rim with ¼- to ½-inch pebbles. Keep the water level in the tray within ½ inch of the surface. This allows the pebbles to remain moist but keeps the water from saturating the bottoms of the pots. The air circulating through this layer of moist pebbles (or gravel) provides humidity for the plants.

Raising the humidity by using pebble trays is not always effective—especially if the air is extremely dry or if there is a lot of air movement around the plants. The bit of moist air from the trays dries up or is circulated away too quickly to be of much help. A solution in this case may be to drape a plastic sheet around the collection, but don't make it too airtight. Some air circulation is required.

Many types of trays are offered by indoor gardening suppliers (see "Orchid Resources," page 92). "Egg-carton" trays are used without pebbles, which makes them easier to clean and carry. A waffle pattern inside the tray holds the pots above the water. You can also place a sheet of half-inch plastic lighting-diffuser grate in the bottom of a tray to create your own egg-carton tray. Diffuser grates are available at most do-it-yourself stores.

Plants are also effective humidifiers. By arranging your orchids in groups with ferns and other moisture-loving plants, you can raise the humidity and, at the same time, create an attractive display.

Ordinary cool-vapor room humidifiers and the more high-tech "ultrasonic" humidifiers are a reliable way to maintain humidity in a plant room or in the area near a plant grouping, perhaps in a fluorescent-light garden. Be fanatical about cleaning the humidifier regularly and, if it has one, replacing the filter as necessary. This prevents potentially harmful bacteria from taking up residence in the humidifier and their possible transmission into the air.

Misting, although commonly practiced, probably provides more enjoyment for the grower than humidity for the plants. If your plants are in an eastern window, a morning spritzing might raise the humidity enough to carry them through the bright morning hours. But in most cases, misting only provides five minutes of relief for a 24-hour problem. It is not a good idea to mist orchid flowers, however, nor is it sound policy to wet the foliage near nightfall. Be

sure that no pools of water are left in leaf centers or other crevices.

You can help maintain humidity by being sure heating vents do not blow directly on your orchids. Draping plastic over a light garden can boost humidity inside.

AIR MOVEMENT

Gentle air movement will help your orchids in many ways. Moving air cools the leaves, allowing the plants to tolerate higher light intensities without burning. It also evaporates water on the surfaces of the leaves and in the cracks between them, reducing the risk of infection by fungi and bacteria. A gentle breeze eliminates pockets of cold air that may form next to the windows or along the floor.

The air movement produced by a ceiling fan mimics the gentle breezes in the leafy canopy of a tropical cloud forest.

The need for ventilation is often emphasized in orchid books written for energy-conscious greenhouse growers, but it is less of a problem for home hobbyists. Still, if your home is very well sealed, indoor pollutants from pilot lights, cooking, smoking, and aerosol sprays can build up to levels that will damage orchid flowers.

Obviously, the easiest way to ventilate a windowsill garden is to open the windows. Don't open them too wide, though, as strong drafts can rapidly dry the plants and a gust of wind can knock them over. Double-hung windows work well because they can be opened from the top, allowing air to circulate through the room without creating drafts blowing directly on the plants.

If it is too hot or too cold to open the windows, circulate the air with a small fan, directed away from the plants. Ceiling fans are quiet, inexpensive to run, and the ideal way to keep the air healthfully activated.

One of the best things you can do for your orchids is to provide them with fresh, moist air that circulates freely. An ordinary oscillating fan placed in the vicinity of your collection is an easy, efficient way to keep the air moving. Gentle breezes reduce disease and foster sturdier growth.

GROWING ORCHIDS OUTDOORS

Any time the weather is warm and frost-free, flowering orchids such as dendrobium and phalaenopsis can be displayed in a sheltered spot.

Lattice panels and fencing with spacing between the boards assure that orchids growing in the area have air.

Orchids can be grown outdoors year-round in some regions of the country. South Florida, all along the Gulf Coast, coastal regions of Southern California, and Hawaii are an orchid grower's dream—many plants can simply be tied to the trees in the backyard. Californians grow cymbidiums in pots on the patio or at the entryway, and San Franciscans and other fog-dwellers have an ideal climate for cool-growing orchids such as odontoglossums and a host of fascinating if relatively small masdevallias.

Across much of the country, orchids can spend the summer outdoors, provided they are not moved until the weather is warm and settled—and they are brought back inside before night temperatures drop below 50° to 60° F. This means that at about the time you plant out tomatoes, eggplants, peppers, and okra, you can safely move your orchid plants to where they will spend the summer. Cymbidiums are an exception to the rule with regard to when they are brought back inside in the fall: Wait until night temperatures hover around 38° to 42° F. This chilling will help set lots of flower buds. The same is true of Christmas, Thanksgiving, and Easter cacti (*Schlumbergera* and *Rhipsalidopsis*).

SUMMERING ORCHIDS OUTDOORS

In areas with warm, humid summers, most orchids will benefit from being placed in the great outdoors, provided they are carefully positioned for healthful amounts of light and given adequate protection against opportunistic insects and other pests, such as slugs and snails. The same as inside, you will need to study how much direct sun reaches any given area. Orchids suited to low light

(see "Ideal Light Ranges in Footcandles," page 7) will adapt well in bright, open shade or on the north side of a wall where the only direct sun is early or late in the day. A site that receives sun in the morning is suited to orchids that thrive in medium light levels, while direct sun through midday and into the afternoon is generally too much even for those tolerant of high light levels. They'll still need some protection (shade trees, shade cloth, or lattice screens) from the sun's hottest rays. Do not move any orchid directly outdoors into full sun; gradually increase the exposure.

ACCOMMODATING ORCHIDS OUTDOORS

While it is possible to hang orchids from tree branches where they will receive dappled sunlight and shade as breezes blow through their leaves, small pots or a large collection can be better managed if you grow the orchids on benches. The surface of the bench needs to be slatted and then covered with quarter-inch wire hardware cloth so that excess water from rain and the hose can rapidly drain off. This arrangement also facilitates free air circulation, which is what orchids are accustomed to in the rain forest.

For maximum comfort, build the benches at a height that suits yours. A tall bench for a short gardener—or vice versa—causes physical stress and also diminishes the sheer pleasure one should gain from growing orchids. Depending on the size of your collection and the various sizes and habits of the plants themselves, you may elect to build some benches more in the style of staging, like bleachers for plants. The lowest may be about 12 inches off the ground, the next stepped back at 24 inches, a third at 36 inches. This arrangement works well set against a wall and may invite installing a shelf on the wall itself about 2 feet above the top "bleacher" shelf. This makes an inviting place to arrange a collection and even though it is essentially an orchid nursery, in its orderliness, there is a certain appeal.

It is not a good idea to set orchid plants directly on the ground. This is a sure way for the pots to become infested with slugs, snails, sowbugs, and other creatures that love the moist environment under the plants and make a meal of your plants in the night.

Never leave an orchid standing outdoors in a saucer or cachepot, which can collect rainwater. Unless you are immediately on hand to empty the excess, the roots will soon perish, and the plant will topple from rot.

In the absence of adequate, regular rainfall, you will need to water your orchid plants

Phalaenopsis and cattleya are displayed in wall-mounted baskets in this shaded garden that features hydrangeas. Quick drainage is essential for orchid pots outdoors.

outdoors with the same devotion you show when they are housebound. Also, maintain your same consistent schedule for fertilizing the plants—this is vital while the orchids are growing outdoors in warm weather. Otherwise, you will be losing an opportunity for them to make stronger-than-ever growth, which helps them prepare to put on the best flower show ever in the next regular blooming season.

Think twice before you put phalaenopsis outdoors. They are vulnerable to sunburn and damage from hard rains and gusty winds. If you have a sheltered porch—ideally a screened one—it could prove a perfect place to summer phalaenopsis outside, along with florist gloxinias and gesneriads, such as African violets. Leave the phalaenopsis on the porch until night temperatures fall to between 50° and 55° F. This slight chill will help the plant set lots of buds for a big show of winter and spring flowers.

BUYING, GROWING, AND CARING FOR ORCHIDS

Your first orchid is likely to be purchased, either by you or by someone who gives it to you as a gift. It will probably be in flower or at least in spike, meaning the buds are about to unfurl, hopefully into glorious bloom. In all likelihood, a flowering-sized orchid will be a better beginning than a seedling or offset that may not attain flowering size for a year or more.

If you have a choice, start with only a few plants representing no more than two or three different kinds of orchids. As a beginner, your chances for success go up if you select from the kinds rated "beginner" in the chart opposite and with the individual orchids discussed in the "Orchid Gallery," beginning on page 56. Build your confidence with orchids from the "beginner" category, then proceed to the "intermediate" and "advanced" categories.

Fortunately, it is the easily grown orchids that are most often available from local sources, particularly the mass merchants. Orchids frequently encountered in such places include phalaenopsis, oncidiums, cymbidiums, and Dendrobium phalaenopsis.

After this introduction, you will be ready for a more sophisticated approach: a visit to a specialist orchid grower or one of the many catalog sources (see "Orchid Resources," page 92). In the long run, your best friends and allies in nurturing your experience as an orchid grower will be the specialists who devote their lives to the art and practice of cultivating orchids. Pass by any suppliers of unknown reputation, those who offer collections of bare-root plants, and avoid like the plague any orchid described as "collected from the wild."

ENDANGERED ORCHIDS

The orchid's popularity has had some unfortunate effects. When the Victorians discovered the beauty of these plants, a huge demand was created. Since there weren't any orchid nurseries with modern propagation facilities, plants had to be collected from the wild. Orchid sellers sponsored plant hunters on expeditions throughout the world. These plant hunters were good—too good—at their jobs, sending back shipments weighing tons and containing thousands of plants. When one of these botanical conquistadors found a valuable species, he took every plant he could find, wreaking ecological havoc. Moreover, only a small fraction of the plants collected survived. Countless species became extinct. Although the number of orchids removed from the wilds for collectors has diminished since the Victorian orchid boom, you still find collected orchids for sale.

■ You can discourage the gathering of wild orchids and their exploitation by purchasing only plants known to have been propagated by legitimate orchid growers. Be careful of advertisements offering orchids described with the words "wild" and "bare root."

■ And remember: The greatest danger to wild orchids is habitat destruction, which destroys all orchids, not just the prettiest. It is estimated that billions of orchids are destroyed yearly by land-clearing operations.

BEGINNER ORCHIDS

Brassavola
Brassia
Cattleya
Cymbidium
Encyclia
Epidendrum
Oncidium
Paphiopedilum (some)
Phalaenopsis

Phalaenopsis
'Candy Stripe'

INTERMEDIATE ORCHIDS

Dendrobium
Laelia
Ludisia
Masdevallia
Miltonia
Odontoglossum
Phragmipedium
Sophronitis (some)
Vanda

Laelia flava

ADVANCED ORCHIDS

Dendrobium (some)
Masdevallia (some)
Odontioda
Paphiopedilum (some)
Sophronitis (some)

Odontioda
Ispann

TYPES OF ORCHIDS

Orchids have two basic growth patterns: monopodial and symmodial. Despite the vastness of the family, most members fall into one or the other category, and none is half-and-half. While different genera of orchids are crossed with each other to create new entities, seemingly with greater abandon than in any other plant family, the bottom line is that monopodials are crossed with monopodials, sympodials with sympodials, but never monopodials with sympodials or vice versa.

Knowing whether the orchid you hold in your hand is monopodial or sympodial is of importance, however, because this information will help you pot and grow it successfully, and it also offers a clue as to how best to propagate the plant.

Ascocenda Su Fun Beauty 'Memoria Jane Figiel' is a notable example of a monopodial orchid. Originated by crossing Vanda × Ascocentrum, the ascocendas are noteworthy for having the most desirable traits of both parents. They bloom generously—as often as three times a year—and are of a conveniently compact size that suits them to the home orchid grower.

MONOPODIAL

A monopodial orchid grows predominantly upward. It has a main stem, which produces new leaves at its tip, and it flowers from buds at the juncture of the recently matured leaves and stem. The word "monopodial" (Latin for "single foot") describes this type of single-stem growth habit. Vanda and phalaenopsis are examples of common monopodial orchids. Other monopodial orchids include aerides, angraecum, ascocenda, ascocentrum, ascofinetia, doritaenopsis, doritis, kagawara, neofinetia, neoaërstylis, and trudelia.

One way to tell the difference between a monopodial and a sympodial orchid is to look around the base where it emerges from the growing medium. If monopodial, there will be no new shoots or baby plants growing up, only the original stalk. By contrast, if sympodial, one or more new shoots can be seen emerging or in

Monopodial

various stages of growth. In nature, both types may seem to move horizontally or vertically away from the point of origination. In cultivation, monopodials—excepting doritaenopsis, doritis, and phalaenopsis—tend to expand upward while the sympodials move horizontally. Doritis, phalaenopsis, and crosses involving both—the progeny of which are known as doritaenopsis—may grow upright for a time, but they will also eventually sprawl across the surface of the growing medium. This appearance usually signals the need to rework and repot the plant to remove the oldest roots and the lowermost stalk from which the oldest leaves may already have matured and dropped off.

Although different monopodial orchids vary in size and potential height, vandas are typical of the largest. Their habit and appearance will vary, depending on whether they are grown in a basket or cradle, without staking or if grown in a pot and staked upright. In either case, the stalk eventually will be bare from the base upward for some distance, with strong, vital air roots issuing all along the way up. At repotting time, the oldest roots and most of the old, bare stalk can be removed, thus bringing the newer, vital parts back down so that they begin or emerge from the growing medium.

If the growing tip of a monopodial orchid is damaged or for some reason removed, one or more new shoots may emerge from the main stalk. After a time, strong roots will grow out from the base of these into the air and when they are at least a couple of inches long, the offshoot can be removed and potted as a new plant.

Monopodial orchids do not have thickened pseudobulbs to store moisture and sustain them through extended dry seasons. They are better suited to a range of moisture between evenly moist to slightly dry rather than any extremes. Especially to be avoided is the state known as "bone dry." If too dry for too long, so that the leaves shrivel, the plant may be unable to assimilate moisture, which means that even if properly watered in the future, it will remain shrunken or unnaturally floppy. Sometimes such a plant can be salvaged by treating the uppermost leaves and stalk as a cutting, set to grow in fresh medium.

SYMPODIAL

A sympodial orchid grows outward along the surface of the growing medium; its stem, called a "rhizome," is often horizontal. New shoots originate from buds on the rhizome and send out their own roots. The flower spikes of sympodial orchids may originate from the base of the plant, usually from the base of a recently matured pseudobulb or from between the leaves at the top.

"Sympodial," Latin for "many footed," describes the spreading growth habit of orchids in this classification. Cattleyas and paphiopedilums are familiar examples of sympodial orchids. In nature, cattleyas are often seen growing on the rough bark of a tree with rhizomes and pseudobulbs spreading outward and upward. When potted, the same cattleyas will move across the surface of the growing medium and, unless repotted into a larger container, will grow over the edge and down the side of the pot or may simply dangle in the air. Paphiopedilums in nature are more likely to occur in pockets of humus and their movement is less obvious since it is more likely to be side-to-side with new shoots arising next to the older ones so that a clump of leaves is formed, oldest at the center, youngest at the perimeter.

Sympodial orchids include species with pseudobulbs that store moisture to sustain them through normal periods of drought but also ones without such moisture reservoirs—

Sympodial

paphiopedilums, for example—which are ill suited to periods of extreme drought, the same as described on the opposite page for monopodial orchids. With a few exceptions, sympodial orchids tend by nature to be better adapted to moisture extremes— especially dryness—than the monopodials. However, even where these are concerned, permitting extreme dryness for too long can result in deeply shriveled pseudobulbs and in withered leaves that then become ill equipped to take up moisture when they are watered or rained upon. Therefore, it pays not to go overboard.

Besides the ever-popular cattleya and lady's slipper paphiopedilum, other sympodial orchids frequently cultivated include aspasia, brassavola, brassia, brassocattleya, brassolaeliocattleya, cattleytonia, cochleanthes, colmanara, cymbidium, dendrobium, encyclia, gomesa, laelia, laeliocattleya, leptotes, lycaste, masdevallia, miltassia, miltonidium, miltonia, miltoniopsis, odontioda, odontocidium, oncidium, otaara, phragmipedium, potinara, psychopsis, yamadara, and zygopetalum.

Cattleya skinneri *shows the growth habit of a typical sympodial orchid, how the rhizome travels horizontally across the surface of the growing medium, rooting as it goes along. Unless repotted, the growing tip will in due course advance over the rim of the pot and down the side— or into thin air— and future growth will be somewhat thwarted.*

TYPES OF ORCHIDS
continued

Most orchids can be classified into one or two of three basic categories according to the conditions under which they or their predecessors have evolved. These include epiphytes (air plants or tree-dwellers), terrestrials (earth plants, plants that grow in soil), and lithophytes (plants whose roots attach themselves to rocks as a means of stabilization).

In nature, the roots of an epiphytic orchid such as Epidendrum nocturnum attach themselves to tree branches and absorb moisture and nutrients from the atmosphere. They are not parasitical.

EPIPHYTES

In the tropics, some orchids live in the humus-rich soil at the edges of streams, in clearings, and other spots on the ground where the dense shade is dappled by patches of sunlight. These orchids are terrestrial, that is, they live on the ground. In most parts of a tropical forest, however, there simply isn't enough sunlight at ground level to support many flowering plants. Thus, most tropical orchids are epiphytes (air plants or tree-dwellers) that have adapted to living up above the ground where the light is more plentiful. When Darwin first saw epiphytic orchids clinging to the branches of their hosts, he thought they were parasites, drawing nourishment from their hosts through tenacious, leechlike roots. This was of course a false assumption; true parasites are rare among plants. Two of the better known examples are mistletoe and a golden yellow, stringlike vine called "dodder."

Actually, orchids use the branches of trees only as a place to live. They absorb their nutrients, not from their hosts, but from the decaying organic matter that accumulates around their roots, and they photosynthesize sugars from the sunlight streaming through the gaps in the leafy canopy. They damage trees only when they grow too heavy for the branches to bear. Occasionally, massive colonies of orchids, often accompanied by ferns, bromeliads, and epiphytic gesneriads, crash to the forest floor.

In adapting to their aerial environment, epiphytic orchids developed thick roots, coated with velamen, a spongy material that allows them to stick to the bark of trees and absorb water rapidly. To survive periods of drought, many species have pseudobulbs, thickened stems that can store both water and food. In other epiphytic species, the leaves themselves are thickened storage organs for water and food.

Epiphytic orchids need to dry out between waterings, briefly in warm, sunny weather when they are in active growth, longer in cool temperatures. Because their pseudobulbs act as storage organs for water and food, epiphytes grow well with less frequent

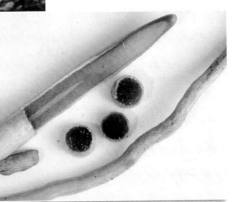

In cross section, the roots of an epiphytic orchid, here a vanda, can be seen to have a silvery white outer layer—a velamen coating that facilitates attachment to an appropriate surface, a tree branch for example, and absorbs moisture and nutrients from the atmosphere. The inner, vascular tissue is vital in the process of photosynthesis, by which the orchid plant is energized.

A terrestrial orchid such as **Spathoglottis plicata** *(from Southeast Asia to the Philippines) is earthbound, usually in moist humus.*

fertilizing than terrestrials. Epiphytic orchids tolerate underwatering better than overwatering; however, inconsistency and extreme dryness are to be avoided. Otherwise the orchid plant may merely exist, almost indefinitely, but it will not bloom and prosper.

There are endless variables, but typically orchids in a home greenhouse require watering and fertilizing twice a week in warm weather, once or less a week in winter. Between waterings in warm, bright weather, leaves and exposed roots benefit from a light misting of water early in the day. Don't leave water standing in the centers of plants or in cupped leaves. It can lead to fungal problems.

TERRESTRIAL ORCHIDS

Most of the terrestrial orchids we grow, such as paphiopedilums, aren't all that different from their tree-dwelling relatives. Because they generally live in rich, fluffy humus, their roots resemble those of epiphytes and have similar needs for water, air, and fertilizer. To further blur the distinction, some epiphytes in their natural state end up living as terrestrials when they fall out of a tree into a sunny spot where there is lots of humus.

Cymbidiums are often classed as "semiterrestrial," a term that helps indicate their adaptability to various growing mediums. Like paphiopedilums, they need perfect drainage and aeration about the roots, yet they also need sufficient humus to maintain a slightly moist condition at all times, never extreme or bone dryness.

While distinctions may blur between epiphytic and terrestrial orchids, in cultivation none is likely to adapt to the

ordinary potting soil used to grow plants such as begonias and geraniums. Soilless mixes that combine peat moss, perlite, and charcoal chips are, however, sometimes combined with bark chips to form a satisfactory growing medium for paphiopedilums and cymbidiums.

Two terrestrials that could never be mistaken for epiphytes are the Australian orchids *Rhizanthella gardneri* and *Cryptanthemis slateri*. These bizarre species grow underground, seeing the light of day only when flowering and dispersing seed. To date, little is known about these oddities.

LITHOPHYTES

Botanical references that discuss the natural habitats of orchids often list an epiphytic species as also being a "lithophyte," which is to say it can be found growing with its roots attached to rocks or growing in extremely rocky terrain where there is scant humus matter. As with an epiphyte, the lithophyte's roots are able to "glue" themselves to the rock surface, but they gain no sustenance from its mineral content. Only from the atmosphere do they absorb nutrients.

Vanda orchids and their relatives such as ascocenda, ascocentrum, and trudelia are sometimes grown in wood boxes or cradles filled with chunks of lava rock. To succeed, they need constant humidity and, especially in warm, sunny weather, to have the roots and rocks drenched with water daily—after which warm breezes quickly dry any excess. This approach to growing these orchids is most often practiced in south Florida and along the Gulf Coast where high humidity goes with the territory and outdoor temperatures are warm enough to sustain growth almost all year, perhaps with a brief time indoors during the coldest of part winter.

When an epiphytic orchid such as **Laelia flava** *is found growing on a rock, it is called a "lithophyte." For an orchid to grow on rocks, constant high humidity is required, along with plenty of rain showers.*

BUYING ORCHIDS

Orchids are available from many sources, but most plants are purchased from flower shops, garden centers, and orchid nurseries. Even grocery stores occasionally have flowering phalaenopsis, cattleyas, dendrobiums, and cymbidiums. Plant nurseries and garden centers are some of the best places for the beginner to shop.

Choose plants with healthy roots, which are plump and silvery white to green. Shriveled, discolored roots indicate the growing medium is decomposing. Also look for unopened buds on the spike. This shows that the plant is beginning to bloom, not finishing up.

The plants you find at local retailers have often been subjected to some fairly trying times due to the distribution system. Look at the leaves. They should be firm and unbroken, but slight damage is no cause for worry. Inspect any visible roots—are they a healthy white with greenish tips? Lift the pot and peek in the holes in the bottom. The potting medium may be slightly decomposed, but you should still be able to make out the individual pieces. Any roots visible through the drainage holes may be dark, but they should not be slimy and rotten.

A plant with an inflorescence (flower cluster) that is beginning to mature is ideal. One or two of the lowest flowers will be open, but the rest should still be in bud. Look carefully at the open flowers. Are they pleasing? Except for slight variations in size and in intensity of colors, the plant will always produce flowers like the ones you are seeing. The main priority, of course, is to select the flowers you like, but it doesn't hurt to consider whether they are good examples of the species or hybrid. This will become more important to you as your collection grows. During this selection process, resist any temptation to reach out and touch the orchid flowers with your fingers. Oils given off by the hands will prematurely age the edges of the orchid flower, causing them to turn brown.

ORDERING BY MAIL

There are hundreds of mail-order orchid nurseries. They range from corporations with sprawling greenhouse complexes and sophisticated ordering and shipping operations to avid orchidophiles who sell a few plants to help offset the cost of their hobby. The big nurseries publish glossy color catalogs. Small firms may send out photocopied pages listing only names and prices. The size of the business doesn't necessarily determine the quality of its plants, but until you become an expert you will need pictures and descriptions to help you make selections. See "Orchid Resources" on page 92 for a list of mail-order nurseries that publish informative catalogs and ship high-quality plants.

Many nurseries offer an orchid-of-the-month program, with selections keyed to your level of experience and your growing conditions. This system will help you maintain a high level of interest, excitement in new arrivals on a regular basis, and a steady increase in know-how without obtaining too many different orchids all at once. It also helps build a collection with blooms all year.

DECIPHERING MAIL-ORDER CATALOGS:
The best orchid catalogs spell everything out: the plant's entire name, its parentage if it is a hybrid, its cultural requirements, stage of growth, plant and pot size, and of course, the price. Other catalogs are more cryptic. In the case of hybrids, the descriptions may not tell what the flowers actually look like, but how the breeder expects (or hopes) they will turn out. Purchasing hybrids that have never bloomed before is a game of chance.

Catalog writers use a number of methods for describing plant size. Most commonly, the size of the pot is listed. To complete the picture, good catalogs will include additional information to indicate what the plants are like in each pot size. "Blooming size" generally means the plant will bloom within a year of purchase, given proper care. For cattleyas and other sympodial orchids, many growers list the number of pseudobulbs. Monopodial orchids are commonly sold by the inch. Phalaenopsis plants, for example, are measured from the tip of one leaf to the tip of the opposite leaf.

If you are a beginner, limit your purchases to mature, blooming-size plants. These usually come in pots 4 inches across or larger. Later, when you have more experience, you can try growing less-expensive, immature plants shipped in community pots (shallow trays containing one to three dozen seedlings) or in small, individual containers.

CARING FOR NEW ARRIVALS

Orchids may be shipped with or without pots depending on the preference of the customer and the practice of the grower. Many people ask for plants to be shipped bare-root to minimize shipping costs and to allow them to pot the plants in their own growing media and containers.

When you receive a bare-root plant, inspect the leaves and roots, cutting off any damaged portions with a sharp, sterile knife. Then pot it and treat it as you would any other newly potted plant.

Potted orchids are allowed to dry out before they are packed so they won't rot in the box. When you receive a potted orchid, inspect the leaves and cut off any damaged parts. Then water the plant. If the pot arrives broken, slip the root ball into a new pot. Unless the roots are badly damaged, you don't need to disturb them.

FINDING BARGAINS

If you are looking for bargains, join an orchid society. At meetings, plants are exchanged in a spirit of appreciation and enjoyment; profit is rarely considered. At these meetings, you may find local growers selling plants at very low prices, as well as a raffle table of plants you might win for a dollar or two. On a less formal basis, society members increase the variety of their collections by trading divisions, seedlings, and keikis (offshoots).

Orchid shows can also be a good source of plants. Although the exquisite specimens in the display area will not be for sale, most shows have areas where growers offer plants for sale at reasonable prices. Usually, the best bargains at these shows are bare-root orchids or recently potted divisions that are fun and exciting to bring home and watch grow.

If purchasing orchids through a mail-order source, the grower will ship them with one or two flowers beginning to open. If buying where you can choose your own plant, select one with more flowers as well as ballooning buds.

WATCH FOR ORCHIDS IN TWO MEDIUMS

If you purchase an orchid—perhaps one in full flower—from an unknown source, check the growing medium when you get home to be sure it is all of one type. Sometimes orchids for the mass market are grown cheek-by-jowl in small pots in the nursery where they are copiously watered and fertilized and pushed to reach flowering size. Immediately before distribution to the retailer, they may be transplanted into a larger pot with a different medium, such as peat moss, or new bark chips added to fill in around the old growing medium. Water such a plant with great care and as soon as flowering finishes, give it a proper repotting.

POTTING ORCHIDS: GROWING MEDIUMS

You will find that the type of container and growing medium you choose will have a great effect on how you care for your plants. At first, keep things simple by using the kind of container and potting medium the plant or parent plant was growing in when you acquired it.

CHOOSING THE RIGHT CONTAINER

Orchids are most often grown in plastic pots. Plastic pots are inexpensive, lightweight, absorb no toxic salts, and retain moisture. Some people prefer the natural look of unglazed clay. Porous clay pots allow the medium to dry out more quickly than it would in a plastic pot—an advantage if you are inclined to overwater. Stick with plastic, however, if you have hard water. The salts in hard water can accumulate in the walls of clay pots and burn the roots.

The roots of some orchids, such as miniature oncidiums, cannot tolerate the moist conditions of a pot, but grow beautifully on slabs of cork, wood, tree-fern fiber, or on branches as in their natural habitats. Colonies of related species are often grown together.

CHOOSING THE RIGHT MEDIUM

Many potting mediums for orchids are available. Over the years, growers have tried everything from exotic fibers to common gravel and from simple mixtures of fir bark and perlite to elaborate combinations. Despite the variety, most growers use fir bark alone or as the main ingredient in a mixture. Commercially prepared mixes are the most convenient for beginners.

FIR BARK: Inexpensive and easy to handle, the rough surfaces of fir bark pieces supply the right combination of air and water to the roots of epiphytic orchids.

Fir bark is available in three grades: fine, medium, and coarse. Fine bark (⅛- to ¼-inch

pieces) is used for seedlings or mericlones, and for mature plants with fine roots, such as miltonias. Medium bark (¼- to ½-inch pieces) is best for most epiphytic orchids. Coarse bark (½- to 1-inch pieces) is right for vandas and large phalaenopsis. Avoid ungraded bark because the small pieces fill in the spaces between the large, resulting in poor aeration. Although fir bark can be used alone, many growers add coarse perlite to increase its water-holding capacity.

As soon as you put fir bark in a pot, it starts to break down. This is its main drawback. As the bark decays, the pieces shrink and settle in the pot. As the pieces get smaller, the spaces between them get smaller too, causing the medium to hold more water and less air. Eventually, if the plant isn't repotted, the roots will rot. Generally, plants in medium and coarse fir bark need repotting every two years, but in humid, warm climates, the bark breaks down rapidly and may need to be replaced annually. Fine fir bark generally lasts about a year, but in warm, humid climates it breaks down far too rapidly to be useful. For

Fir-bark chips

Peat moss

Tree-fern fiber

RECIPES FOR FAVORITE MIXES

GROWING MEDIUM A is typical of all-purpose media sold at nurseries for epiphytic orchids. It consists of 1 part perlite, 1 part coarse sphagnum peat moss, 6 parts coniferous bark (fir, for example), and 1 part horticultural charcoal chips.

GROWING MEDIUM B is designed for terrestrial orchids grown in pots, cymbidiums for example. It consists of equal parts garden loam, sphagnum peat moss, and clean, sharp sand. An alternative is to mix together by volume 2 parts of a purchased soilless medium such as Pro-Mix with 1 part bark chips.

GROWING MEDIUM C is a finer version of Mix A, for seedlings and orchids having delicate roots. Mix 6 parts fine bark chips, 3 parts sphagnum peat moss, and 3 parts chopped live sphagnum moss.

this reason, most orchid growers in Florida use a more stable medium such as tree-fern fiber.

The organisms responsible for the decay of bark use a great deal of nitrogen. If there isn't enough nitrogen for the decay organisms and the plant, the plant suffers. You can't stop the decay, but you can easily compensate for it by using a high-nitrogen fertilizer, such as 30-10-10, to fertilize plants potted in fir bark.

TREE-FERN FIBER: The second most popular potting medium for orchids is tree-fern fiber. Its resistance to decay and excellent aeration make it the preferred medium in Florida, where the year-round warm temperatures and high humidity quickly rot fir bark. The disadvantages of tree fern are its relatively high cost and low water retention; tree fern costs about twice as much as fir bark and needs to be watered twice as often. To overcome these problems, many tree-fern users mix in some coarse fir bark.

Because tree fern breaks down so slowly, balanced fertilizers such as 23-19-17 or 20-20-20 are recommended.

REDWOOD BARK: Similar to fir bark, redwood bark offers the advantage of decay resistance. Although it comes from California, most redwood bark is used in Florida, where it lasts even longer than tree fern. It is often used as a component in mixtures. Use a balanced fertilizer for plants in redwood bark.

OSMUNDA FIBER: This fiber comes from the roots of ferns in the genus *Osmunda*. At one time, it was the most popular medium for orchid culture. It has become so expensive, hardly anyone uses it anymore. Fir bark seems to work as well, is easier to handle, and is much less expensive.

COCONUT-HUSK FIBER: This by-product of coconut processing is relatively plentiful and, when dry, quite lightweight so that it can be shipped efficiently. The pale, reddish brown color flatters the green of orchid plants and looks attractive in either clay or plastic pots. It works well as the sole medium for epiphytic orchids and is slow to decompose. Balanced fertilizers such as 23-19-17 or timed-release 14-14-14 work well with coconut fiber.

CHARCOAL: Hardwood charcoal (not pressed-powder briquettes like you use for barbecuing) is added most often to cork or redwood bark, both of which produce a lot of acid. Charcoal absorbs the acids. It is also a common component of commercially packaged mixes. Like lava, charcoal collects salts, so don't use it if you have hard water.

GRAVEL: Despite its advantage of absolute decay resistance, gravel is rarely used because it holds little water or nutrients, is very heavy, and can tear the roots from plants when they are eventually repotted.

LAVA ROCK: Plants growing in lava rock can remain undisturbed for many years because lava does not decay. Lava is well aerated and retains water well, though not as satisfactorily as fir bark. Its main disadvantage is its tendency to accumulate salts; don't use lava if your water contains large amounts of dissolved minerals. Lava is most commonly used in Hawaii, where its low cost and high resistance to decay make it the medium of preference. A 20-20-20 fertilizer works well with lava.

MAN-MADE MEDIUMS: These include a variety of products made from clay or shale that have been fired to form nuggets of a porous material similar to lava rock. Expanded clay is most commonly used in Hawaii, with balanced fertilizer such as 20-20-20.

PERLITE: This processed volcanic material is used as an additive to other potting mediums. Perlite's low cost, high water-holding capacity, and decay resistance make it a popular additive to fir bark.

SPHAGNUM MOSS: This comes in several forms: long or short fibers, alive or dried. Live sphagnum is best for orchids, and most expensive. It is green, and, if not overwatered or over-fertilized, it will continue to live and grow after it is placed in the pot. It is used most often as an additive to other potting mediums, though some growers use it alone for special plants in small pots, or to nurse ailing plants back to health.

CORK: Crushed cork is usually mixed in nearly equal parts with charcoal for potting orchids, and has a small but loyal following. Whole wine corks are too large and dry for use as a potting medium.

PEAT MOSS: Peat moss has an even greater water-holding capacity than sphagnum, but it decomposes more rapidly. Coarse peat was once a favorite ingredient in orchid mixes, but it has become scarce and expensive and is now rarely used. It should not be mixed with tree fern, cork, or osmunda fiber, but may be blended with fir bark or charcoal. Coarse peat moss contains few nutrients and breaks down slowly, so balanced fertilizers are recommended. Horticultural peat is too fine and dense for orchids.

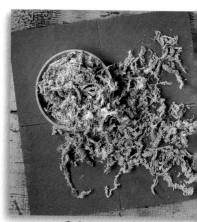

Sphagnum moss

Coconut-husk fiber

Osmunda fiber

Coarse perlite

POTTING ORCHIDS: STEP BY STEP

Sooner or later, every orchid needs repotting. Like other houseplants, orchids should be moved to larger pots as they grow. Repotting is also the first step in nursing an overwatered orchid back to health. More often, the growing medium decays and restricts the flow of air to the orchid's roots before it has outgrown its container. In this case, the plant is often repotted back into its original container with fresh medium.

WHEN TO REPOT

Unless you are trying to save a sick or damaged orchid, wait to repot until after flowering—the time most orchids begin a cycle of root growth. Orchids repotted at this stage are quick to reestablish.

The new roots in sympodial orchids are usually obvious, at the base of the new growths when the shoot is a couple of inches long, or from the newest part of the plant before the new shoot appears. New roots in monopodial orchids may not be as readily apparent, but they usually begin growing as soon as flowering finishes.

In any case, repot when the new roots first appear. Once the roots have grown more than ½ inch, they are easily broken during transplanting. If damaged, young orchid roots won't grow again until the next year.

HOW TO REPOT

When you repot an orchid, remove all the growing medium from the roots, leaving them bare. This may seem to be an overly drastic treatment, but if you don't remove all the mix

TESTING THE SIZE OF A POT

The next pot for a sympodial orchid needs to accommodate two years' new growth. Judge by placing the oldest pseudobulb against the rim to see if there is enough room in front for the youngest shoot to expand. Select the next pot for a monopodial orchid so that it is only large enough to hold the roots without bending or breaking them. Be sure to avoid overpotting.

from the roots, it will continue to decay and could eventually lead to root rot.

You will need a sharp knife with a long blade, pruning shears, a blunt dowel or stick, and, of course, the potting mix. Sterilize all cutting tools to prevent the spread of viruses. Before working on each plant, hold the blade in a flame, such as from a propane torch with a piezoelectric starter, for several seconds.

■ **WATER THE ORCHID.** A thorough watering makes the roots easier to handle.

Center a monopodial orchid in the pot with the bottom of the lowest leaf at the bark surface, ½ inch below the pot rim. Position a sympodial orchid plant with the oldest pseudobulbs against the rim and the newest growth aimed at the rim on the opposite side of the pot.

POTTING TIPS

Potting an orchid is fun. You get to hold the plant, look at it from all sides, and prune and wash the roots. Here are some tips to help you master this enjoyable process:

■ Sift or wash the splinters and dust out of fir bark or tree fern before use. Otherwise, the smallest particles will settle to the bottom of the pot and clog the air spaces.

■ Always sterilize tools with a propane torch before working on each plant to avoid spreading viral diseases from one plant to another.

■ Place a plastic bag over a newly potted plant to help maintain humidity. To allow some air flow, don't close the bag completely, and cut a few small holes in the plastic on all sides of the plant. Don't allow direct sunlight to strike the covered plant—the trapped heat will roast it.

■ Never use ordinary, all-purpose potting soil for orchids.

■ Label plants immediately after potting them, otherwise names and tags are easily lost and often impossible to match up again.

■ Cymbidium pseudobulbs are held close together by tough rhizomes. Bend and twist the bulbs apart to separate them, then cut through the rhizome with a knife.

■ To pot successfully, let this be your motto: *Make haste with deliberate slowness.*

■ **REMOVE THE PLANT FROM THE POT.** Lay the pot on its side, grasp the plant at its base and tug gently. The root ball of a terrestrial will usually slide right out, but the roots of epiphytes often cling to the container. If the plant won't come out with a gentle tug, work a long-bladed knife around the inside, between the pot and the roots. Then turn the pot back on its side, grasp the root ball as before, and gently tug the plant out of the pot. If it still won't come out—sometimes the case with cymbidiums in clay pots—break the pot by tapping it lightly with a hammer.

■ **CLEAN THE ROOTS.** Shake the old potting medium from the roots. Wash away the clinging bits with water. Cut off any rotten roots (black or dark brown; some portions may have sloughed away, leaving only the threadlike center). Leave the healthy roots intact unless they have grown outside the pot and would be broken off in repotting. If this is the case, cut them back to 3 or 4 inches long.

■ **POT THE PLANT.**
SYMPODIALS: Hold the plant in position with the oldest pseudobulbs against the rim. Adjust the height of the plant in the pot so that the base of the rhizome is about ½ inch below the rim. If the new growth is higher than the old pseudobulbs, position the plant at an angle so that it is growing parallel to the bottom of the pot. Fill in bark around the roots, firmly tamping it in with your fingers or a dowel. After adding a few handfuls, lift the pot and thump it back down to settle the bark. Continue adding bark until it covers the sides of the rhizome. Thump the pot again.
MONOPODIALS: Center the plant in the pot (if it is tall, place a stake next to it at this time). Position the plant so the bottom of the lowest leaf is at the surface of the bark—about ½ inch below the rim of the pot. If the lowest leaf doesn't have at least three healthy roots on the stem below it, strip off one or more of the bottom leaves until there are healthy roots that you can anchor in the bark. Cut off the very bottom of the stem if it doesn't have roots on it. Fill in bark around the roots, tamping it with your fingers or the dowel. After each handful, thump the bottom of the pot against the table to settle the bark. Continue adding bark until it reaches the bottom of the lowest leaf. Thump the pot again to settle everything in place.

■ **SUPPORT THE PLANT.** Top-heavy orchids such as cattleyas need to be supported with a stake to keep them from toppling. Other orchids with large root systems can stand on their own. Metal stakes that clip to the side of the pot work best. Clip the stake to the pot at the back of the plant and tie the pseudobulbs to it, using raffia, garden twine, or plastic-coated telephone wire. Rhizome clips designed to anchor the plant in the medium are also available from orchid supply companies (see "Orchid Resources," page 92).

You can settle the new growing medium around an orchid's roots by tamping and poking gingerly with a dowel, but your fingers are the most sensitive—and convenient.

ORCHIDS ON SLABS: MIMICKING MOTHER NATURE

One of the most fascinating ways to grow orchids is to attach the plants to slabs of cork bark or tree-fern fiber. Until the roots of the orchid become established, it is necessary to attach the plant to the mount by the use of monofilament fishing line, twine, wire, staples, or even instant glue. Electrician's staples work well; their flat tops make them easy to press into the wood or cork, and it doesn't take long for a layer of rust to form so that they blend into the background.

In addition to fishing line, staples, or another means of attaching the orchid, you'll need a fresh slab of cork bark or tree fern, some sphagnum moss, and a pair of pliers. Always wear gloves when handling sphagnum moss. Despite the fact that this product of the earth was once considered sterile enough to bind the wounds of Civil War soldiers, it is now known to occasionally harbor a fungus that can cause serious illness in humans.

Start the mount by making a small, slim pad (about the same diameter as the plant) out of the sphagnum moss. Staple the pad to the cork bark or tree fern and put the plant on top of it, arranging the roots so they extend outward. Fasten the roots to the mount, putting small rolled-up pieces of moss between them and the staples or wire. In very humid or wet conditions, attach the plants directly to the slab without the bottom pad of moss. Keep the plants lightly shaded and water them infrequently until they become established. This usually takes six to eight weeks. Light misting daily through this period will help speed the establishment process.

Most mounts last a long time. You won't need to transplant the orchids until they begin to hang off the sides. Even then, if the mount is in good condition, you can allow the plants to continue growing undisturbed by attaching the overgrown slab to the center of a larger one of the same material. If the oldest parts of the orchid plant begin to die off in the center, it is time to salvage the healthiest parts and establish them on fresh mounts.

Mounted orchids generally do best if situated where the air is buoyant and full of moisture. They tend to become too dry in the window of an average home. Interior situations better suited include sunrooms and other plant-dedicated rooms, window and home greenhouses, and conservatories.

POST-PLANTING CARE

When you finish potting and staking any orchid or attaching it to a mount, move the plant to a slightly shadier location than it grew in before. Make sure the air is adequately humid, but withhold water or water very sparingly for one to two weeks to give the roots and stems a chance to heal. Daily misting will help. Water the plant less frequently than usual for the next two months to stimulate root growth, and fertilize it lightly when you water. After four to six weeks, you can move the orchid back into brighter light and begin to treat it as usual.

Attach moss

Spread out roots

Tie in place

10 ORCHIDS TO GROW ON SLABS

Brassavola nodosa
Dendrobium
Encyclia
Epidendrum
Masdevallia
Oncidium
Ornithocephalus
Psygmorchis pusilla
Sophronitis acuensis
Trichocidium 'Elvena'

Brassavola nodosa *is especially attractive growing on a bark mount. In summer, hang the plant outside near a sitting area, where its exquisite scent can perfume the evening air.*

STAKING

Although staking may be no more than a common-sense means of protecting a developing spike of orchid flowers while the plant is in transit, it can also be a happy marriage of art and science that results in a subtly more beautiful presentation at flowering time. Orchid growers use galvanized wire stakes in a variety of configurations that come preformed to suit the habits and various sizes of the most commonly cultivated orchids. Three types offered for sale where orchid plants are sold include:

■ A length of straight wire, usually 12 to 18 inches long, with its top bent into a U-shape. The "U" holds the flowering spike and the effect of the stake is based on its depth, angle, and positioning in the growing medium.

■ A wire with one end shaped to clip over the rim of the pot, above which a length of straight wire—usually about 5 to 8 inches tall—extends. The upper end of the wire is formed into a circle that can be from 4 to 5 inches in diameter or up to 8 or 10 inches across. This circle is intended to cradle several or many mature growths of cattleyas and similar orchids.

■ A wire pot clip, which is hardly more than a horizontal length of wire, usually 4 to 8 inches long, with bends in one end to clip over the pot rim. This simple piece of equipment is used primarily to secure sympodial orchids after they are first potted, until the roots become established.

Another type of stake used by commercial growers is bamboo, which can be thin and reedlike or as thick as a pencil. Sometimes these stakes are inserted only to protect the orchid during shipping, with no particular concern as to whether or not the size is aesthetically pleasing or in relation to that of the orchid plant itself.

On other occasions, the bamboo cane that comes with a purchased orchid needs no further dressing other than to have utilitarian plastic ties or twist-ties removed and replaced with the more graceful and organic raffia. Be gentle when tying the orchid to the stake. Use a figure-eight tie, first wrapping the raffia tightly around the stake, then loosely around the orchid stem.

Besides wire and bamboo, a third material for staking orchids can be found in most yards, namely twigs from trees and shrubs. Often these can be cut and trimmed so that a "Y" or "U" already present in the branches can gently cradle and hold the orchid spike to show off its beauty to maximum advantage.

One pitfall in staking orchids lies in installing the stake. It's easier than you think for the medium to resist your attempts to insert the stake. In response, you may push harder until something gives or breaks. You can hurt yourself this way, but more likely your hands will come crashing down and break off one or more buds or flowers, if not the entire spike. Go easy!

SOME MATERIALS FOR STAKING

Bamboo canes
Twigs
Wire: orchid flower stakes
Wire: orchid plant stakes
Pot clips
Raffia

Three staking methods (left to right): wire, cane and raffia, and twig. Inset: raffia in bow tie.

To keep cymbidium leaves separate and symmetrical, they can be tied individually but connected by using a single long piece of raffia.

Use lemon juice to remove spray residue and water spots, leaving orchid leaves clean and shiny.

GROWING ORCHIDS: WATERING

Use the pencil test: Sharpen a pencil to expose new wood. Insert it into the medium about 1 inch deep and twist a few times. If the wood comes out damp, water is not needed. If it is dry, your orchid probably needs watering.

Put the right orchid in the right light in the right growing medium in the right range of temperatures and all that remains for a resounding success are the right watering and right fertilizing practices. The one inviolate rule about watering is never leave an orchid standing in water. Another is to avoid overwatering the plants.

Beginning orchid growers, assuming that tropical plants need to be kept continuously wet, often overwater their orchids. Although it is true that the forest habitats of many of our most treasured orchids are moist, the plants themselves grow in some of the driest spots in these forests—in the trees. Because there is no soil to hold moisture for them between rainstorms, epiphytic orchids have evolved special roots that enable them to capture and retain the water that briefly falls on them. These roots are sheathed with velamen, a white, spongy material that absorbs moisture from rain or dew and holds it until it is drawn into the pseudobulbs and leaves.

Orchid roots don't just need water—they also need air. When the velamen on a root remains saturated for too long, the inside of the root suffocates and begins to rot. Thus, although velamen performs a positive function for a plant on a tree, it can be a liability for a plant in an overwatered pot.

Some beginning orchid growers are alarmed to find their plants sending roots straight out into the open air. This is natural. They may look a bit unruly, but you'll probably soon agree that these roots add to the plants' charm. They should not be cut off, forced into the medium, or otherwise disturbed.

WHEN TO WATER

How can you tell when to water? There are many variables: Some types of orchids require more water than others, and some have rest periods when they should receive little or no water. These specifics are described for each type of plant in the "Orchid Gallery," beginning on page 56. Also, the type of pot and growing medium the plant is in will influence its need for water, as will the light intensity and other environmental factors discussed earlier. Despite these factors and exceptions, it is still possible to offer a few general (and generally safe) guidelines.

WATERING TIPS

The old expression, "He who holds the hose, grows the rose," also applies to orchids, but only to the extent that proper watering is the key to success. Here are some suggestions to help you master this all-important aspect of orchid care.

■ Before you water a plant, lift the pot to see how much it weighs. With some practice, you will be able to tell whether the plant needs water simply by hefting it.

■ Water your plants in the morning so that the excess water will evaporate rapidly.

■ All other things being equal, plants in clay pots or small pots will generally require water more often than will plants in plastic pots or large pots.

■ You can tell if a pseudobulbous orchid is receiving enough water by looking at the pseudobulbs. The youngest pseudobulb should remain plump, but the older ones may shrink slightly between waterings without harm.

■ As a potting medium ages, the air spaces in it shrink, making it retain more water. Thus, newly repotted plants need to be watered more often than those that have been in the same growing medium for a while. In a collection of many plants, it will help at watering time if those in aged potting medium are separated from those that have been recently potted.

■ Epiphytic orchids with pseudobulbs or orchids with very succulent leaves should be watered when the potting medium is almost completely dry. To test for dryness, press your finger about one knuckle deep into the medium. If it feels moist, wait a day or two and test it again before watering it. If it is dry to the touch, the plant should be watered.

If you prefer not to put your finger in the pot, use a pencil. Sharpen the pencil to expose new wood, then insert it into the medium and twist it a few times. If the wood is damp, you don't need to water the plant.

■ Orchids without pseudobulbs or succulent leaves, such as paphiopedilums and phalaenopsis, should not be allowed to dry out completely between waterings. Test these plants before watering them as you would an epiphytic orchid, but water them when the medium is still slightly moist.

■ You will find that high temperatures, bright light, low humidity, and fast air movement will, singly or in combination, increase an orchid's needs for water. By keeping an eye on your plants' growing conditions, you will soon learn how frequently you need to water them. You will probably find that you'll water most of your plants about once a week in winter, twice or more in summer, especially if they are outdoors.

This cattleya orchid shows by its overall shriveled and shrunken state that it has been habitually underwatered. Gradual, slow rehydration could save it.

Conversely, this orchid appears to be badly in need of water when in fact its roots have all died from prolonged overwatering. It may not be salvageable.

HOW TO WATER

When it's time to water an orchid, water it thoroughly. If possible, take the plant to the sink or bathtub and pour plenty of water through the potting medium. This thorough soaking will flush any accumulated salts out of the pot and will provide the even moisture that encourages large, healthy root systems. Use room-temperature water if possible—cold water may invigorate people, but it shocks plant roots and can damage the leaves of orchids such as phalaenopsis.

If the water in your area is hard—that is, full of dissolved minerals—flush the plants out with distilled water (or rainwater) every so often to keep the minerals from building up in the potting medium. Never use water that has been chemically softened—the sodium in this water will quickly kill the plants.

When watering an orchid, it is vital that water be applied over the entire exposed surface area, not in one spot alone. This is because of the relative coarseness of the media used to grow orchids and the fact that they do not "wick" water throughout the pot like regular houseplant potting soils that contain peat moss and other humus.

A policy that will help you water your orchids effectively is to group the pots by size and kind of orchid. Sometimes a collection will grow like Topsy, with little pots jammed

next to big ones, where they can be easily forgotten at watering time (and possibly robbed of light). Conversely, when orchid plants of different kinds, sizes, and in different types of pots—clay, plastic, wood slat—are mixed together on a table or bench, you may be tempted to water them all the same. This will not produce uniformly beautiful and thriving orchid plants. It is better policy to group plants of a kind as well as pots of the same type and size so that their watering needs—as well as light needs—can be more precisely judged and little left to guesswork.

Orchids on slabs require special care at watering time. In a greenhouse, they can be hosed down. In the house, they need a brief dunking or shower from a kitchen sink hose sprayer.

GROWING ORCHIDS: FERTILIZING

In the wild, epiphytic orchids obtain nutrients from the decaying organic debris that collects around their roots. Terrestrial orchids obtain nutrients from the organic matter on the ground. The plants do not absorb nutrients directly from organic matter. They depend on bacteria to break it down and liberate its constituents in simple forms the plants can readily absorb. As long as the temperature is warm enough to keep the bacteria active, they produce a continuous, though dilute, supply of nutrients. Your orchids will grow best if you mimic this natural process by fertilizing them frequently with a dilute fertilizer solution. Luckily, you don't have to brew a concoction of dead leaves, bird droppings, and insect bodies to feed your plants—other equally effective and much more convenient fertilizers are available.

An orchid such as this **Cattleya bicolor** *'Measuresiana' will have more and larger flowers if the plant is well nourished.*

TYPES OF FERTILIZERS

Fertilizers may be organic (derived from plants and animals) or inorganic (derived from minerals). The nutrient content of both types is described by a set of three numbers on the label. These numbers indicate the percentages of nitrogen, phosphorus, and potassium—in that order—in the fertilizer. For example, a fertilizer labeled 15-5-5 contains 15 percent nitrogen, 5 percent phosphorus, and 5 percent potassium. Some fertilizers also contain trace elements such as iron and zinc. These are equally as important to healthy growth and flowering as are the well-known nitrogen, phosphorus, and potassium. Plants simply don't need as much of them.

The type of fertilizer you choose depends mainly on the medium in which your plants are growing. Orchids growing in bark need much more nitrogen than phosphorus and potassium because the bark decays so rapidly. Although one would think the decaying bark would provide nitrogen for the plants, it

Dry or blackened leaf tips on an orchid plant are a sign of too much rather than not enough fertilizer. Drench the medium with fresh water several times to help rinse out the fertilizer excesses.

FERTILIZER TIPS

■ Most fertilizer problems result from too much rather than too little fertilizer. Keep in mind that in the wild, orchids grow in a lean regime. If the tips of the leaves become dry and blackened, you may be overfertilizing. Cut off the burned tips with sterilized scissors and pour plenty of fresh water through the medium to flush out the excess fertilizer. If the symptoms are severe, repot the plant with fresh medium regardless of the time of year.
■ Fertilize only when the plants are actively growing—in other words, fertilize only when the season and growing conditions are conducive to active growth.
■ Always use a measuring spoon when adding fertilizer; guessing leads to overfertilizing!

■ Don't fertilize plants suffering from too little water or damaged roots. Water them with plain water until they recover.
■ Water plants immediately before fertilizing to prevent injury from fertilizer salts. Resist the urge to "push" your plants with extra fertilizer. Extra fertilizer actually stunts plants.
■ It is generally thought that it is better to fertilize orchids with nitrogen derived from sources other than urea. If in doubt about the source, read the label on the container.
■ Until you settle on one or more fertilizers that give you the results you want with your orchids, try products labeled specifically for orchids or purchase the fertilizers sold by specialist orchid growers.

actually does the opposite. The bacteria that break down the bark take most of the nitrogen for their own use, leaving little for the orchids. For this reason, orchids planted in bark should be fed with a fertilizer containing a high ratio of nitrogen to phosphorus and potassium, such as 30-10-10 or 15-5-5. Note that these formulations have the same ratios of nitrogen, phosphorus, and potassium (3:1:1). The first formulation is simply twice as concentrated.

Fish emulsion labeled 5-1-1 is a popular organic fertilizer for orchids grown in a greenhouse, but its strong odor makes it unsuitable for home use. Plants growing in tree-fern fiber or other relatively stable materials do well with a balanced inorganic fertilizer such as 20-20-20 or 23-19-17. These are offered by many companies; the best also contain iron and other trace elements.

Many growers alternate fertilizers, switching to a low-nitrogen, high-phosphorus fertilizer (such as 10-30-20) to stimulate flowering when the plants complete their vegetative growth. While not absolutely necessary, this practice may improve the quality and number of flowers.

Time-release fertilizers are sometimes used for orchids growing outdoors in summer or in a greenhouse where temperatures are controlled thermostatically around the year, or in fluorescent-light gardens where the amount of light is constant and not influenced by the time of year or by periods of cloudy weather. Osmocote 14-14-14, for example, is excellent for orchids growing in tree-fern fiber or other stable materials. Read the product label so you'll know when to re-fertilize; some pellets release nutrients for a period of 90 days, others for 120 days. Scatter the pellets uniformly over the surface of the growing medium, not all in one spot.

HOW TO FERTILIZE

"Weekly, weakly" aptly describes the constant feeding regime that works best for orchids. It is also the easiest way to make sure your plants are adequately fed. Each time you water your plants, or with one watering each week, give them a half-strength fertilizer solution. (Half-strength is one half of the rate recommended on the label for potted plants.) However, if you have hard (highly alkaline) water, add fertilizer to the water every other time you water. The alternating plain waterings flush out excess minerals.

If you are growing orchids on bark mounts, remove them from where they hang and dip the plant, mount and all, in a pail of fertilizer solution. Dip up and down a couple of times, remove and let the excess drip off and then

Guess which orchid plant has been fertilized regularly. It's the healthy one on the right, of course, and it will also be the one to flower sooner with more blossoms than the undernourished one on the left.

hang the plant back where it has been growing. If you are afraid of spreading disease by dipping more than one plant in the solution, an alternative approach is to spray bark-mounted orchids with fertilizer solution. If you have only a few plants, use a hand-operated, pistol-grip mister. If you have many, in a greenhouse or outdoors for example, use a pressurized sprayer dedicated to this use, one in which a weed killer has *never* been used.

PROMOTING FLOWERING

Most orchids will flower on their own without any special treatment, as long as they are receiving adequate sunlight and proper temperatures. Some species, such as the deciduous dendrobiums, need seasonal treatments to promote flowering. These usually involve cutting back on water and fertilizer to respect the plant's resting period—the period following a cycle of vegetative growth. It is impossible to say how long the resting treatment should last in terms of weeks or months—the requirements of the different species and the conditions under which they can be grown vary too much. Generally, you should allow the orchid to rest from the time its newest growth has matured until it starts to produce new growth or flower spikes. For specific recommendations on the rest requirements of orchids, look under the genus in question in the "Orchid Gallery," beginning on page 56.

DIVIDING AND REPOTTING ORCHIDS

Orchids can be propagated both sexually and asexually. Division is the simplest and most popular method and, because it is asexual, it is a reliable way to have more plants of a favorite orchid that will grow up to be exactly the same. Division is typically a part of the repotting process, although there is no law against impulsively offering a division of an admired plant to a friend who is visiting, presuming the orchid has multiplied to the point of being divisible. In this case—and depending on the growth habit of the orchid—the offset may be removable along with a promising set of roots without greatly disturbing the parent. In some cases, though, it may be wiser to unpot the orchid, shake away the growing medium, and proceed with division in the accepted manner. One of the orchid plant's advantages in this sort of transaction is that the offset can simply have its roots and rhizomes or pseudobulbs wrapped loosely in moistened paper towels and the whole dropped in a plastic bag for traveling to its new home and proper potting up.

This sympodial orchid has long since outgrown its pot. To avoid long-term decline, it needs dividing and repotting into as many as three or even a half dozen vigorous new plants.

PLANT DIVISION

Many orchids are easily propagated by division, a process of splitting a plant into two or more actively growing pieces at repotting time. In "Potting Orchids: Step-by-Step" on page 28 are instructions for producing a few large divisions. When propagating, however, you usually want to produce as many new plants as possible, so the techniques are a little different.

Dividing the plant is optional. If it is growing in a fine, symmetrical pattern and is producing new growth from several points, you probably won't want to divide it because it is on the way to becoming a spectacular specimen. But if it has grown in a straight line across the pot, died out in the center, or has some other defect, you can improve its appearance and stimulate new, more promising growth by dividing it.

More often than not, you will want to divide the plant in order to propagate it. The techniques for dividing sympodial orchids are different from those used for monopodial orchids; be sure to follow the instructions pertaining to the type of orchid you have (see photos on pages 20 to 21).

■ **SYMPODIALS:** To divide a sympodial orchid plant, cut it into sections by slicing through the rhizome (the horizontal stem joining the pseudobulbs) with a sterile knife or shears. Leave at least three leafy growths on each section, preferably four or five.

When a sympodial orchid has grown in a more-or-less straight line across the pot, it can be made more attractive by dividing and repotting to produce a more rounded plant.

When a sympodial orchid plant has been in the same pot for a long time and has multiplied around the edges, its dead center is a clarion call for a makeover and repotting.

Normally, if you are dividing the orchid at the same time as you are repotting it to develop a specimen plant or to improve the habit of the plant, you will remove and discard all of the leafless, shriveled pseudobulbs and preserve all the healthy ones intact. These supply food to the rest of the plant and may sprout new growth.

If you are dividing and repotting solely to propagate a sympodial orchid into as many new growths as possible, start by following the directions for repotting. Then, divide the plant into portions containing a minimum of three leafy pseudobulbs and plant these divisions in separate pots of appropriate sizes.

In this case, however, *don't* discard the dormant pseudobulbs you removed from the active growths; these can be used to make new plants. Strip away the old leaf bases if present and plant the pseudobulbs in moist, live sphagnum moss or fine bark with the "eyes" (dormant buds) above the surface of the medium. Place them in a warm area and keep the moss or bark moist but not soggy. When the buds sprout new growth, gradually acclimate the plants to the growing conditions of the mature plants. They will reach blooming size in one to three years.

Old pseudobulbs can be rehabilitated in any growing situation where temperatures are comfortably warm for you in your pajamas (65° to 80° F) and light is bright but there is not much direct sun. A warm fluorescent-light garden where the air is moist and buoyant can be ideal, as can a propagation corner set aside in a home greenhouse.

■ **SIMILAR ORCHIDS:** Paphiopedilums don't have pseudobulbs, but their growths are connected by a rhizome. Thus, you divide a paphiopedilum in the same manner as you would a sympodial with pseudobulbs, cutting through the rhizome to create divisions with at least three leafy growths each.

Two orchids that are grown for their beautiful leaves, *Ludisia discolor* var. *dawsoniana* and *Macodes petola*, are described in references as being terrestrial and growing from creeping rhizomes. Neither is called "sympodial," though technically they may be. Pieces of ludisia stem, if broken off and inserted in live sphagnum moss and perlite, kept nicely moist and in high humidity, will root and form new plants. This is unusual for an orchid, but it shows almost anything is possible within this varied family.

■ **MONOPODIALS:** Because sympodial orchids tend to multiply into clumps that in some ways resemble common garden plants such as bearded iris, they often seem easier to propagate than the monopodial orchids, such as vanda and ascocentrum. However, these plants can also be multiplied in a variety of ways, usually by observing what is going on with each plant.

Typically, an older monopodial plant will grow tall and somewhat leggy, with a portion of stem toward its bottom that is leafless. The plant can be shortened by cutting off its top immediately below a node with well-developed aerial roots. The upper part is then potted separately while the old plant, though leafless or nearly so, is returned to where it has been growing. It will usually produce new growth at the top of the cut stem, which later can be removed and planted. Or, it may sprout new growth at the base of the stem. If that happens, the old stem can be cut off once the new growth is well established.

If an older, leggy, monopodial orchid plant is lacking aerial roots, which facilitate shortening and thereby jump-starting the parent plant into producing new top growths or basal shoots, try this air-layering procedure: Wrap a handful of moist, live sphagnum moss around a portion of the bare stem, covering at least two or three nodes where leaves once grew. Enclose the moss in plastic. When roots have begun to grow actively into the moss, the stem can be cut directly beneath the air-layer and potted as described on pages 28 and 29.

One aspect of nurturing orchid plants is that at repotting time it is necessary to sort through the roots one by one and trim out any that are dead or damaged. Work carefully and you will be well rewarded.

DIVIDING AND REPOTTING ORCHIDS
Continued

At repotting time, cut out every dead, rotted, and broken root. Also, remove the oldest, leafless, shriveled pseudobulbs. Sterilize pruners before using on another orchid plant.

If you have a choice, never divide and repot an orchid while it is actively growing, in the process of sending up flower spikes, or actually flowering. The ideal moment for dividing an orchid is at the very outset of a new growing season when the new roots are barely beginning to appear. Fortunately, not all orchids will reach the perfect stage for repotting at the same time—some are better repotted in the fall, others in late winter or spring. When you reach the state of having a sizable collection, the differing needs of orchids themselves will help you spread your work load so that it doesn't become burdensome.

If you find it necessary to repot an orchid after it is well along in new growth or a spike has begun to emerge, be forewarned: New shoots on orchids—whether leaves or flowers—are extremely tender, and vulnerable to the slightest bruise or misplaced movement. It is almost impossible to not break off something you desperately don't want to lose if you try to divide and repot an orchid that has already advanced into fully active growth.

Young orchid plants often benefit from being moved to a pot that is a size or two larger at the beginning of each growing season. Most mature orchids need repotting only once every two years, or before the growing medium begins to decompose. Cymbidiums and restrepias are examples of orchids that may require repotting no more often than once in three or four years. The leafy calanthes and phaius may benefit from repotting almost every year.

It is always a good idea to keep records for each orchid plant as to when it was repotted. Do this with indelible ink on a label placed in the pot. If you are a meticulous record keeper, further notes may be kept by assigning a master number to each orchid plant, which corresponds to the same number kept in a notebook or, more likely, in a computer data file. In your main database, you can list the orchid's full name, the date it was obtained, from whom, and any other information you may have gleaned about it.

The records you keep in a notebook or your computer are actually much more reliable than what is placed in the pot. Plastic labels, almost universally used today, have the unfortunate trait of growing brittle from exposure to sunlight and hot and cold temperatures. Typically, one will snap in two when you are busy caring for the orchid and, in haste, push the two pieces together between the growing medium and the wall of the pot. Before long—unless you are a highly disciplined person—the pieces will become separated and you will have to become something of a sleuth to figure out everything you'd like to know about the orchid's family tree. Assigning a number to the orchid will make it somewhat easier to keep track of the plant. In fact, you might even want to write the number on the bottom of the pot with a bold, indelible magic marker. Note: The ultra-fine point permanent markers that many of us use are not reliable for labels. Indelible is something of a misnomer when they are used for plant labels because repeated exposure to the elements fades the ink in months, until it becomes illegible.

DON'T OVERCROWD

One of the most fundamental rules for success in developing an orchid collection is one you may rarely, if ever, read anywhere but here: You must be disciplined about the number of plants you try to house in your accommodations. More collections have been spoiled by overcrowding than almost any other practice or condition. Overcrowding thwarts air circulation, prevents the orchid plants from developing symmetrically, and encourages all manner of insect pests and diseases. Too many plants can also have a depressing effect on the would-be orchidist and instead of being a mood elevator, can actually induce the opposite effect as you contemplate all the work they require.

There are basically two ways to end up having entirely too many orchids: One is to buy indiscriminately until push comes to shove, especially at the moment of truth in fall, when all frost-tender plants must come inside. The other is that you cannot bear to discard any division or keikis that appears on

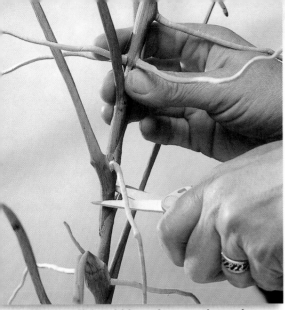

Monopodial orchids such as vanda can be propagated by cutting off the top of the plant beneath several aerial roots and potting it up separately. The old plant will also sprout anew.

place where it will have the chance of growing to perfection.

Another practice that will help you have a successful collection that is pleasing to the eyes—even when not in bloom—is to arrange orchids of a kind together, as well as to arrange them by pot kind and size. These practices are not only visually calming in their repetitiveness, they also help you take better care of your orchids. If different kinds and sizes are all mixed together, the hodgepodge is visually chaotic and proper care is almost impossible, especially with regard to watering and fertilizing.

You will enjoy the work of dividing and repotting your orchids more if you organize a potting bench that suits your height and work habits. Back and shoulder aches as well as tendonitis—"tennis elbow"—are aggravated by work surfaces that are mere inches too high or too low. The quality of your work and the pleasure you take in it will also be affected by having good light and, if you need it, a magnifying glass to bring small things up close and into sharp focus. Add to these basics a supply of clean, fresh pots in different sizes, growing mediums, staking and tying materials, and you will be a most happy orchidist.

your potting bench when repotting or in the process of staking and grooming.

If you want to have a truly beautiful and soul-satisfying collection of orchids, you must discipline yourself to buy only those plants without which you cannot be happy. Don't acquire one more plant unless you have a

SEPARATING NEW AIRBORNE PLANTS

One of the marvels of monopodial orchids such as vanda, ascocenda, ascocentrum, and trudelia is that a mature plant or one with a damaged growing tip will often sprout "babies" from along the main stem. These resemble the keikis associated with phalaenopsis in that they form new plants with leaves and roots in the air on the old stems.

When these offsets are large enough to handle, with roots at least 2 inches long, they can be cut from the parent stem with a knife or merely removed by hand with a slight twisting or downward movement. Then, the "baby" plant is ready to be set into its own small pot of fresh growing medium. It will likely reach flowering size in one to three years, and the flowers will be exactly like those of the parent plant. The ideal time to remove such an offset from a monopodial orchid is at the beginning of the most active growing season, usually in late winter or early spring. The parent may yield more offsets later if it is encouraged to grow.

Sympodial orchids such as cattleya and dendrobium often produce new offsets that either stand above the old growths— with their roots extending down all around—or, in the case of dendrobiums, baby plants form along the old canes. In fact, if nobile dendrobiums are haphazardly cared for in the fall—watered when they should be dry, or kept warm when they need to be cool—the flower buds will often abort and become new plants. In any event, when these growths have a promising set of roots and the leaves are expanding rapidly, they can be cut or broken from the parent and potted separately. Late winter and spring are usually the times to take advantage of these growths, although they can be successful at almost any season in a fluorescent-light garden where temperatures and humidity are always favorable. Flowering size can be reached in about two seasons, and the offsets will produce leaves and flowers exactly like those of the plant from which they were taken.

PROPAGATION

Offshoots, commonly called keikis (their Hawaiian name, pronounced "key-key"), are small plants produced at the base or along the stems of monopodials, or from the pseudobulbs of some sympodials. The leaves of a keikis form first, followed by the roots. When the roots are between 1 and 2 inches long, twist or cut the keikis off and plant it separately in fine bark. Under good growing conditions, a keikis will reach flowering size within two years.

Phalaenopsis plants sprout keikis from buds along the flower stem and because they do this quite commonly, it is a capability most often associated with them rather than the orchid world at large. These fledgling plants can be removed from the parent when they have well-developed roots. Treat them like other types of keikis. If the roots aren't coming along, encourage them by bending the flower stem down and planting the keikis in a pot of bark. Once the keikis has rooted into the bark, cut it free from the flower stem and the plant will rapidly develop.

Select a mature dendrobium cane that has not flowered. Cut it off at the base, then cut it into 4- to 6-inch sections, each with two or three nodes where leaves once grew. Lay the cuttings on damp, long-fiber, live sphagnum moss and cover with glass or plastic. Keep moist. New roots and leaves will sprout from the nodes.

Dip stem cuttings of dendrobium in fungicide before laying them horizontally on sterile sphagnum moss to root.

MERISTEM CLONING

The techniques of propagating by division and by keikis work on a small scale, but they are far too limited for commercial growers, who need to produce as many plants as

When a keikis or offshoot is well-formed on phalaenopsis, cut or break it from the main stem.

Set the keikis to grow in fresh potting mix, the same as any orchid of the same type. If a keikis forms leaves but no roots, draw it down to a pot of fine bark, anchor the base, and roots will grow.

possible as quickly as possible. Meristem cloning (usually shortened to "mericloning" or "meristemming") is a tissue-culture technique that allows them to meet this challenge, producing thousands of plants from a single superior specimen.

The two most important events in the the twentieth century world of orchids have been the discovery of growing seeds in a sterile agar solution and the advent of tissue culturing. Before these two events, orchids were propagated so slowly and, in many ways, so mysteriously that there was little hope of them becoming one of the world's most popular flowers, as they are today. Fine orchids would still be rare and very expensive.

Although mericloning is complicated and requires some expensive equipment, the basics are fascinating and worth knowing. Most hybrid plants are produced this way, starting out as tiny lumps of tissue swirling in flasks of sterile nutrient solution.

Suppose an orchid breeder has painstakingly nurtured a hundred seedlings from a cross and found—years after the flower was pollinated—that one of the offspring has spectacular flowers. In addition to being beautiful, this new hybrid is valuable— enough that the grower will go to a great deal of trouble to propagate it for sale.

To start the process, the plant is taken to an antiseptically clean laboratory where the tip of one of the shoots is removed. Working with a scalpel and microscope in a chamber designed to exclude airborne fungi and bacteria, a technician carefully strips the embryonic leaves from this shoot tip. Removing the tiny leaves reveals the meristem, a primal lump of actively growing cells less than ½ millimeter in diameter. Meristems are like embryos, capable of growing and changing into the cells that form leaves, stems, roots, and, eventually, flowers.

The meristem is placed in a flask of nutrient solution, which is then put into a climate-controlled chamber where it is gently agitated by a machine. The lump grows other lumps, which are removed and placed in other flasks. These lumps generate more lumps, which are also removed and put into flasks. This process of orchid fission continues until hundreds—sometimes thousands—of embryonic orchids are swirling in flasks.

When enough lumps have been produced, they are planted into flasks containing solid nutrient medium. There they develop into tiny plants with leaves, stems, and roots. Eventually the plants grow large enough to be transplanted into the open air. Several years later, these clones may be found flowering on windowsills and in greenhouses throughout the world.

The practice of meristemming has led to a new way of selling orchids. Typically, a flowering specimen will be displayed in the greenhouse sales area and all around it will be seemingly countless small pots of clones. While the flowering plant is not for sale—or if so, only at a high price—the clones are reasonably priced and the purchaser has every assurance that each and every one will grow up to be as fine as the parent.

Mericlones of an orchid species are often made from a choice selection that is finer than a run-of-the-mill example of the type. It may have larger and more flowers, greater vigor, more compact growth, or better foliage. All of these possibilities are taken into consideration before an orchid grower goes to the expense of meristemming thousands of replicate baby plants.

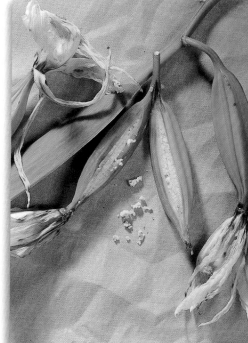

Each orchid seed pod contains millions of dust-sized seeds.

ORCHIDS FROM FLASKS

Some nurseries offer flasks of orchid seedlings growing in nutrient jelly (sterile agar). Although they are relatively inexpensive, they are extremely tender and a challenge for even a veteran orchid grower. If, however, you have a greenhouse, or space under fluorescent lights, you may find it highly rewarding to obtain a flask of seedlings and grow them, first transplanting to community pots, then later to individual pots. It may take three to five years for the first blooms to appear. Depending on the cross, it is always possible you will find a winner among your flasklings, in which case all the trouble will seem worth it. A standard reference for handling flask seedlings is Rebecca Tyson Northen's book, *Home Orchid Growing*.

While mericloned orchids are almost always from superior parents, orchid seedlings, which result from sexual propagation, can run the gamut from inferior to extraordinary.

Tiny orchid seeds must be sprouted in flasks of sterile agar solution. They take four to seven years to reach flowering size and will vary even if from a single species.

ORCHID PROBLEMS

Spider mites stipple leaf undersides and create gossamer webbing.

Orchids are tough plants, resistant to insects and diseases, and capable of enduring a considerable amount of environmental stress. But if a plant's natural defenses are weakened by adverse growing conditions, it may succumb to opportunistic pests. The key to growing healthy orchids is to avoid stressing them.

As it turns out, most orchid stress is related to water—either too much or too little of it. Too much water in the soil rots roots. Standing water—whether around roots or on leaves and petals—encourages infection by bacteria and fungi. Because of its role in life processes, too little water—in the soil or the air—especially stresses plants, and water-stressed orchids are an invitation to scale insects and mealybugs.

This may appear to be a no-win situation, but keep in mind that these are the extremes. Many orchids can withstand long periods of drought without harm, and when growing in the proper potting medium, they can tolerate a great deal of moisture.

Aside from minimizing stress, you can also prevent problems by keeping the plants and their growing area clean. Fungi form millions of spores on dead leaves and flowers, so remove any dead material as soon as you notice it. The papery sheath covering pseudobulbs provides a perfect place for scale insects and mealybugs. Leave sheaths on new growth, but remove them as soon as they dry out and peel away from the pseudobulb. Remove dead leaf tips with scissors or shears, making the cut about ¼ of an inch into healthy tissue. To avoid transmitting viral diseases, sterilize the shears between cuts.

DIAGNOSING PROBLEMS

Your first step in diagnosing a problem is to understand the growing conditions the plant prefers. Then, while inspecting an ailing plant, compare what it needs to what it's getting. In this way, you often can predict the cause before you find it. You'll also be better able to sort out whether the problem results from an insect, a disease, or improper culture. As you inspect the plant, use a magnifying glass to find small pests, such as mites. Be sure to also check the roots of an ailing plant.

When treating plants, be aware that few pesticide products are registered for use on indoor plants. Check the pesticide label; if it does not allow indoor use, take plants outside to spray them and leave them outside until the spray has dried. Also check labels to ensure the product can be used on orchids to control the pest in question. You should be able to find pesticides for use indoors from orchid suppliers and retailers who specialize in houseplants.

INSECT PESTS

PEST: SPIDER MITES. Rapidly moving yellow, green, or red specks on lower leaf surfaces. It takes a magnifying glass to see them.
SYMPTOMS: Stippling on the undersides of leaves, sometimes also on the buds and flowers, and fine webbing.
TREATMENT: Mites thrive in dust so keep leaves clean. Occasionally wash plants with warm water and liquid detergent to prevent outbreaks. For infested plants, spray leaves, especially the undersides, with insecticidal soap. Treat plants weekly for several weeks to kill mites as they hatch. To avoid introducing mites to your collection, carefully inspect new plants before bringing them in.

Aphids favor new leaf and flower buds.

A severe infestation of scale on an orchid stem

Boisduval scale on a leaf

PEST: APHIDS. Small (less than ⅛ inch), slow-moving, soft-bodied, green, yellow, or pink insects that cluster on new growth, flowers, or flower buds. Cymbidiums are especially susceptible.
SYMPTOMS: Buds, flowers, and tender new growth look pitted or stunted. Honeydew, a sticky fluid secreted by the insects, provides a medium for growth of sooty mold, which attracts ants and looks like a black fungus.
TREATMENT: Spray with insecticidal soap, Orthene, diazinon, carbaryl, or malathion. For minor infestations, simply remove insects by washing plants with warm water and detergent.

PEST: MEALYBUGS. Oval to elliptical, cottony-appearing insects with threadlike legs around their horizontally ridged body.
SYMPTOMS: Mealybugs quickly form colonies on leaf and petal undersides, in crevices between leaves, and inside bud sheaths. In time, they develop a cottony

coating, hence the nickname "cottony mealybug."
TREATMENT: Physically remove them using a cotton swab dipped in denatured alcohol. Repeat every five to seven days until close inspection shows the plant is clean. Weekly sprays with insecticidal soap, carbaryl, Orthene, diazinon, or malathion are also effective.

PEST: SCALE INSECTS. Hard-shelled, immobile, brown, white, or grey bumps attached to leaves, stems, pseudobulbs, and flowers. Several types of scale insects attack orchids, including common brown and Boisduval scales.
SYMPTOMS: Scale insects are elliptical to round bumps, ¹⁄₁₆- to ⅛-inch long. Severe infestations can scar and stunt the plant. Like aphids, scale insects secrete honeydew so sooty mold and ants may tip you off to their presence.
TREATMENT: Remove scales with a swab dipped in denatured alcohol. Inspect plants often, removing scales as you find them. Control severe infestations by spraying with insecticidal soap, Orthene, carbaryl, diazinon, or malathion. Spraying is most effective against the tiny young scales (crawlers), which have no shells and move about the plant or from one plant to another. Spray plants weekly for several weeks to kill crawlers as they hatch.

PEST: SLUGS AND SNAILS.
SYMPTOMS: Chewed leaf and petal margins, holes in buds, slime trails over flowers and other surfaces.
TREATMENT: Remove and destroy these pests. Check under pots and rims; be fiendish about litter removal. Use slug bait for large outbreaks.

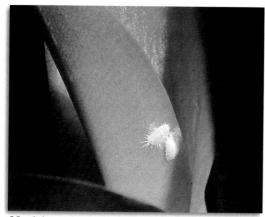
Mealybugs look cottony.

Slugs nibble and leave slimy trails.

DISEASES

Black rot begins on leaves or new growth and spreads into the rhizomes and roots. Treat it as soon as it is observed.

Orchids are not by nature disease prone. However, if they are crowded so that air can't freely circulate between plants, they're more likely to have problems. Orchids growing in decorative nondraining cachepots are especially vulnerable to root rots. Avert disaster by setting the orchid in its pot on a small, overturned pot in the bottom of the cachepot. Excess water then collects below the orchid's roots.

Sanitation and providing good growing conditions are the keys to controlling diseases on orchids indoors because, as with insecticides, few fungicides are available to nonprofessionals and even fewer products can be used indoors. When selecting a product, read the label carefully to ensure that it is labeled for indoor use on orchids and that it controls the disease in question.

ROTS

DISEASE: BLACK ROT FUNGUS, *Phytophthora cactorum* or *Pythium ultimum.* Cattleyas and phalaenopsis are especially susceptible, but dendrobiums, oncidiums, and vandas can also get the disease—as can any orchid left standing in water or in actively decomposing growing medium.

Root-rot fungus spoils the roots, spreads through the pseudobulbs, and results in overall shrinkage and yellowing of the foliage before it too succumbs. Treat plants at once.

SYMPTOMS: Soft, rotted areas begin on leaves or new growth, then spread into rhizomes and roots and to other leaves if not checked. Infected leaf areas initially are purplish brown, turning black. The advancing front of the spreading disease is yellowish.

TREATMENT: Remove infected areas, cutting half an inch into healthy tissue. Sterilize the cutting tool in a flame after each cut. Take the plant outside and drench it with a fungicide containing etridiazole or copper sulfate. Isolate the plant in a low-humidity area to dry off. Water carefully until the plant recovers.

DISEASE: ROOT-ROT FUNGUS, *Fusarium oxysporum cattleyae* or *Rhizoctonia solani.*
SYMPTOMS: The plant wilts because roots have rotted. Brown, rotten areas may extend from the roots into the rhizomes. Leaves become yellowed and twisted.
TREATMENT: Cut off all rotted roots and discolored rhizomes, sterilizing the blade between cuts. Repot the plant, using new medium and a sterile pot. Take the plant outside and drench it with a fungicide, one containing benomyl if possible; it can be hard to find. Follow all instructions on the label.

DISEASE: BACTERIAL BROWN SPOT, *Pseudomonas cattleyae.* This is the most common disease of phalaenopsis, but it is known to infect other types of orchids as well.
SYMPTOMS: A sunken, water-soaked lesion develops on the leaf, which eventually turns brown or black. The lesion exudes dark liquid.
TREATMENT: Remove badly infected leaves, sterilizing shears between cuts. Spray the plant

Bacterial brown spot reduces the leaf to yellow, then to squishy brown. This disease often makes its appearance first in a young pseudobulb (inset) such as that of a miltassia.

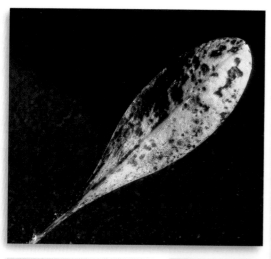

Petal blight or botrytis causes spots, blotches, and prematurely browned petal and sepal edges.

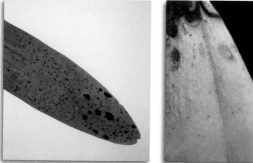

Several fungal leaf-spot diseases attack orchids. Typically, they begin as yellow areas on the leaf undersides, but as they darken, the spots are visible on both sides. Good culture, air circulation, and hygiene help prevent them.

TREATMENT: Cut off and destroy all affected flowers. Increase air circulation and lower humidity, if possible. Clean up any decaying plant matter or litter in the area that may harbor the fungus. Avoid splashing flowers when watering plants.

VIRUSES

DISEASE: VIRUSES. Many viral diseases infect orchids, but diagnosis is difficult. Symptoms can resemble less serious problems.
SYMPTOMS: Black, red, or yellow spots or streaks on leaves. Flowers may have white or brown streaks or mosaic patterns.
TREATMENT: Viruses are incurable; destroy infected plants. Plants may carry viruses without symptoms, so sterilize tools in between use on each plant. Space plants so that they don't touch.

Many viruses infect orchids. Symptoms appear on flowers (as in cymbidium mosaic on cattleya, left) or on leaves (tobacco mosaic on potinara, top right and yellows on vanilla, bottom right).

with a bactericide. Because the exudate contains bacteria, isolate infected plants to keep the disease from spreading. Discard plants if their crowns are affected.

SPOTS

DISEASE: LEAF SPOT FUNGUS, *Cercospora, Colletotrichum,* and other fungi.
SYMPTOMS: Spots start out as yellow areas on the undersides of leaves. As they develop, they become visible on both sides of the leaf and turn purplish brown or black.
TREATMENT: Spray plants using a fungicide containing benomyl, if available. Remove badly damaged leaves. You can leave the ones with a few spots.

BLIGHTS

DISEASE: PETAL BLIGHT, *Botrytis cinerea.* This is one of the most common diseases in indoor and outdoor gardens. On orchids, it's usually only a problem in humid greenhouses.
SYMPTOMS: Small, circular, pinkish or tan spots appear on sepals or petals after flowers open.

CULTURAL PROBLEMS

Probably no one who successfully grows orchids has done so without solving some problems along the way. It helps if you can get into the role of sleuth. To do this, you will need a good magnifying glass. Surely that fictional orchid grower Nero Wolfe had one for his detective work, which he must also have used at home to diagnose orchid problems as well as to better appreciate the finer points of the blossoms.

To be your own orchid problem-solver, practice being a keen observer. Examine the troubled plant in good work light, the sort a dentist or doctor uses, and, if you need them, use your best reading glasses. To comprehend what you see, it will be necessary to know the growing conditions needed by the type of orchid you are inspecting.

OVERWATERING: Often cited as the most common problem with orchids, overwatering results in pseudobulbs (and leaves, if succulent) that are shriveled and growing slowly or not at all. Inspect the roots and you will find evidence of rot. The treatment is to reduce watering or to repot if the medium has decayed. Keep the plant shaded in a humid area until new roots become established.

Sometimes this condition is the result of planting in a pot that is too large and in which the medium has begun to decompose. Again, the solution is to repot, this time into a smaller pot, using fresh medium.

UNDERWATERING: Possibly the second most common problem with orchids, underwatering has symptoms exactly the same as overwatering—with one important exception: The roots will be firm and white when you inspect them. The treatment in this situation is to water the plant several times in succession until the medium is soaked. The pseudobulbs should plump up in a day or two. In the future, water more frequently. However, if you wait to water an orchid until it has dried out completely, the roots may not be able to quickly take up moisture. Frequent watering, then, can lead to root rot.

Shriveled pseudobulb from underwatering

OVERFERTILIZATION: This condition can occur from too-frequent applications or from haphazard measuring. Symptoms include leaf edges and tips that are burned and roots that are withered, especially at the tips. Treat by leaching out the fertilizer by pouring several gallons of plain water—deionized if you can find it—through the growing medium.

Mineral deposits

SCALY OR POWDERY WHITE MINERAL DEPOSITS: Found on the rims and exterior walls of a pot and on the surface of the medium, these deposits indicate that your water contains high concentrations of minerals. Leaf tips may show signs of being burned by excess salts, and new growth may be stunted. The solution: Pour several gallons of plain or deionized water through the medium to leach salts. Or repot the plant. When you water, do so thoroughly over the entire surface of the growing medium, not in one spot alone. If your water is extremely hard, mix it with deionized water or rainwater to reduce the concentration of minerals.

TOP-HEAVY PLANT IN SMALL POT: This is an obvious visual clue that it's time to divide and repot an orchid plant. The less obvious symptoms include gradual, even yellowing of the leaves, the oldest affected first. There may be an overall dullness about the appearance of the foliage. New growth likely will be stunted and the pseudobulbs will extend out over the edges of the pot, or be packed to the point of beginning to grow on top of each other.

SUNBURN OR TOO MUCH LIGHT: Sunburn is indicated by scorched blotches on leaves and exposed surfaces of pseudobulbs, or a general, overall yellowing of the plant. In extreme cases, the flower buds may be deformed. Provide less light, more shade, lower daytime temperature, or increase humidity and improve air movement to prevent heat buildup.

TOO LITTLE LIGHT: Inadequate light is indicated by foliage that is unnaturally dark green but otherwise healthy and a plant that remains flowerless. Increase light gradually over a period of a month. If the plant is growing under fluorescent lights, increase the number of lamps, replace them if they have been in constant use for a year or more, raise the plants so that they are closer to the light, or increase the number of hours the lights are turned on each day. However, don't light the plants for longer than 14 to 16 hours a day.

AIR POLLUTION: Certain types of air pollution can be a problem if not detected and corrected. Gases in the air—ethylene from ripening fruit, sulfur dioxide from smog, and other gases from pilot lights, stoves, or heaters—can result in flower damage ranging from drying and discoloring of the tips of the sepals to rapid wilting of the flower. Buds may fall off. Sheaths may yellow and dry before buds appear. Don't leave flowering orchids in a closed room with ripe apples or hyacinth flowers; both give off large amounts of ethylene. Improve ventilation and make sure gas appliances are properly adjusted.

BUD DROP: Bud drop can be caused by temperature fluctuations, reduced humidity, or

Bud drop from air pollution

a change in environment—as well as air pollution. A large swing in temperature in a brief period, for example 20° F or more, is one of the most common causes of bud drop. Also, moving an orchid in bud from ideal light, moisture, and temperatures, such as in a greenhouse, sunroom, or light garden, to a relatively dark, dry, home situation may also result in buds shriveling and dropping. It's better to wait until flowers have opened before moving plants.

PLEATED LEAVES: This condition occurs among orchids having relatively thin leaves, miltonia for example, and orchid plants that in general are weak, stunted, and shriveled. Pleated leaves are a signal of inadequate watering.

If the growing medium dries too much between waterings, roots never have a chance to become sufficiently established to boost

Pleated leaves

vigorous growth. All they are doing is surviving. Water more often. Be consistent. Mark your calendar if you have to, then keep appointments with your orchids the same as you do your friends and business associates.

Another possible cause for pleated leaves and overall lackluster plants is too little of the good things orchids need, namely, a moist atmosphere and fairly strong light. It may be that you need to add a cool-vapor humidifier to your growing area during that time of the year when the heating system is being used, along with some fluorescent or other supplementary lights.

LACK OF REST: This can keep orchids from thriving in the same way it can cause humans to malfunction. It is more likely to be a problem if plants are growing under lights, in which case, use a timer to assure they receive uniform amounts of light and dark over each 24-hour period. Leaving the lights on nonstop is just as detrimental as leaving the orchids in total darkness for a similar period.

Potted too high

POTTED TOO HIGH: Particularly with phalaenopsis, doritis, and doritaenopsis, an otherwise healthy plant may develop shriveled leaves. Check to be sure that it is not set too high in the growing medium. If you see that the lowermost leaf is an inch or more from the surface of the medium, replanting is in order so that the bottom leaf emerges from the stem at the surface of the medium rather than above it. Remove the plant and do a complete repotting. Do not attempt simply to push it down into the existing old medium.

WEEDS: These can be a problem with a collection of potted orchids, because there are several endemic to the orchid world that aren't going to go away any time soon. *Oxalis acetosella* is one; another is a small acanthus with big roots, such as a *Chamaeranthemum*. The cure for weeds is persistence in pulling them, along with their roots, as soon as you notice them.

Fern "weeds" crowding an orchid

ODDITIES: Within the world of orchids, there are some species having such an unusual appearance that could fool you into thinking something is amiss. For example, consider the *Restrepia xanthophthalma*, whose tiny flowers appear on top of the leaves. Now is the time to use that magnifying glass for something more rewarding than looking for trouble!

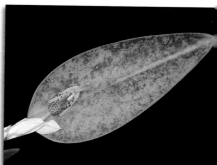
Restrepia xanthophthalma

ORCHID
BOTANY AND
NOMENCLATURE

Epidendrum macrochilum roseum *became available to gardeners in 1844.*

Orchid history is filled with the adventures of "jungle" explorers, controversial theories posed by eccentric botanists, and sensational stories that rival modern-day reports of alien visitors.

Captivating in their beauty and fascinating in their complexity, orchids are easily the most colorful and intricate of all flowering plants. In the early nineteenth century when the plants were first discovered by British horticulturists, people became so taken with orchids that they reached a state popularly described as an orchidelirium, an ecstatic near-madness, an obsession in the truest sense of the word. At that time, orchids were thought by some to have a mysteriously seductive animal essence. Others attributed the flowers' appeal to their sublime beauty.

The original fascination with orchids started in 1818 with the well-publicized blooming of a spectacular lavender *Cattleya*, the forerunner of today's corsage orchids. The demand for these exotic and beautiful flowers was so great that orchids became big business almost overnight. Wealthy collectors and commercial nurserymen commissioned professional plant explorers to gather plants from equatorial regions around the world. Thousands of plants were collected and sent to Europe where, because of the huge demand, they were sold for exorbitant prices.

The plant explorers endured many hardships—dangerous voyages, hostile cultures, thieves, and exotic diseases—but the orchids and the trees that bore them suffered far worse. To attain their prizes, the hunters chopped down entire trees, stripped the orchids from the fallen branches, and packed the plants into crates. The crates were then hauled to the nearest port where they often sat for days or even weeks before being stacked into the dark, dank holds of ships. Once aboard, the orchids had to endure long voyages on the high seas to England, France, and even the United States.

Not surprisingly, few of the plants survived these voyages. Those that lived long enough to reach the greenhouses of collectors were subjected to the most trying of growing conditions. Before the mid-1800s most orchid growers shared the misconception that their plants had been gathered from dark, steamy jungles. When the plants arrived, growers put the orchids in "stove houses," steamy greenhouses heated to unbearable temperatures by coal-, or wood-burning stoves, which required a man to keep them going at all hours. They thought that this duplicated the natural conditions. No ventilation was provided for fear the steam and heat would escape. To us, this kind of treatment hardly seems favorable to any kind of life, but at that time, people rarely ventilated their own living spaces, believing that drafts of air led to a number of fatal diseases. Against such odds, even the toughest orchids hardly had a chance, certainly not those from more mountainous, higher altitudes that were adapted to relatively cool nights.

As proof of their enduring nature, enough orchids did survive and bloom to fuel the Victorian demand for more plants. For over a hundred years, orchid hobbyists and their suppliers spent fortunes sponsoring explorers

2580. Oncidium ornithorhynchum. (×¼)

From Central America: **Oncidium ornithorhynchum**

in search of new species—species they could name after themselves, their friends, and their families. The not-so-privileged public was also fascinated by orchids, and crowds flocked to orchid shows, lured by the imaginative stories of writers such as H.G. Wells, who portrayed orchids as sinister plants with a thirst for human blood.

This mania wasn't just a Victorian fad. The mystique of orchid growing, combined with the endless possibilities of hybridization, continues to enthrall hobbyists around the world. Today professionals sometimes pay

thousands of dollars for an irresistible trendsetter. Orchid societies meet regularly throughout the world to trade plants and tips, and their dazzling shows of artfully composed, if unnatural landscapes, filled with stunning hybrids outshine the wildest dreams of the Victorians.

ORCHID HABITAT

Orchids are found all over the world, in all but the harshest climates of permanent frost or unrelieved aridity. As many as 35,000 species have been named so far, and new ones continue to be discovered every year. About 150 of these species are native to North America. Europe is home to a similar number of species. Although another 500 different orchids hail from Australia, by far the majority live in the tropical regions of Central and South America, Africa, Madagascar, Asia, and New Guinea.

While North America is home to relatively few orchid species, the North American cypripediums are prized by orchid fanciers around the world. The pink lady's slipper, *Cypripedium acaule* (USDA cold hardiness zones 5 to 7) and yellow lady's slipper *C. calceolus* var. *pubescens* (USDA cold hardiness zones 5 to 8) represent two of the most beautiful of all woodland natives. They have a similar appearance, except for the color of the flowers. However, their pH requirements are quite different: Pink lady's slipper does best in a decidedly acidic range of pH 3.5 to 5; yellow lady's slipper thrives in a pH range of 5.5 to 7. Both are protected by the Endangered Species Act.

First collected in Malaysia, Dendrobium farmerii, *appeared in the garden world in 1849.*

will thrive with a treat-
t to *Dendrobium*. A. cor-
lightful fragrance when in
ar to that of the tuberose.
and flower, if cut off from
what it receives from the
er, flourish so well in this
basket, having a mixture of
able mould at the bottom.
aced in the baskets, spread
bots, and hang them up to
a few twigs, formed as the
CRA COCCINEA is a splendid
ts beautiful crimson flowers
l manner: but it flowers
oss be tied round the stems,
np. After it comes into
down, and hung up in a
ng house, where, if treated
continue for a long time.
y cuttings.

Early garden books recommended growing dendrobiums and other orchids in twig baskets.

ORCHID BOTANY

Why all the fuss over orchids? They are obviously beautiful, but so are many other flowers. What makes orchids so special? Part of it is a mystery, simply an unexplainable emotional reaction, but part is based in science. As botanists will explain, orchid flowers are the most advanced and intricate in the entire plant kingdom. In their evolution, orchids have become specialized, developing complex and effective mechanisms that induce insects and other animals to pollinate their blossoms.

Perhaps the bee is attracted to **Dendrobium crumenatum** *by the scent of its flowers, which last only one day. The species is from Southeast Asia.*

PARTS OF THE ORCHID FLOWER

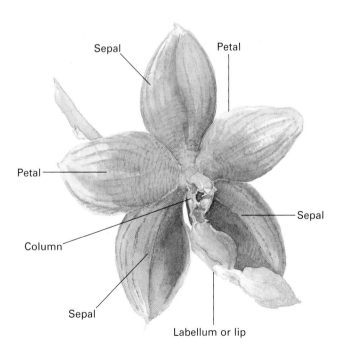

Sepal

Petal

Petal

Sepal

Column

Sepal

Labellum or lip

BOTANICAL SOPHISTICATION

Charles Darwin observed that the nectar produced by the flowers of *Angraecum sesquipedale* (from Madagascar) was held at the bottom of a long, pointed tube, far out of the reach of any insect he had ever seen. Assuming that this nectar attracted pollinators as it does in other flowers, he postulated that angraecum flowers must be pollinated by a "huge moth, with a wonderfully long proboscis" able to tap the nectar. Forty years later, Darwin was proved correct when scientists on Madagascar found the very moths he had envisaged.

This was the beginning. As more orchids were studied, botanists were astounded by the variety and sophistication of their colors and structures. They were amazed by the way some orchids mimic the appearance and odors of female insects in order to inspire the amorous attentions of males—a phenomenon delicately dubbed "pseudocopulation." Orchids in the genus *Ophrys* seem to have perfected this seductive mimicry, enhancing their uncanny resemblance to female wasps or flies with a fragrance nearly identical to the insects' sex attractant. But when a male attempts to mate with one of these flowers, all it gets for its trouble are pollinia (clumps of pollen) to transfer to another flower where the insect is duped again.

OTHER TRICKS: Not all orchid mimicry is seductive. Some oncidium species challenge the territorial instincts of bees by dangling their threatening (to the bees, anyway) flowers at the ends of long, slender stalks, a trick botanists call "pseudoantagonism." When the flowers move in the breeze, the bees attack. After furiously bumping the flowers like airborne bulls, the bees come away with wads of pollen stuck to their foreheads, pollen they can't help but transfer to other flowers in ensuing battles.

Some paphiopedilums pander to the appetites of flies with the foul (but luckily faint) fragrances of rotting fruit or meat. Brown, green, and purple petals with fuzzy black warts resembling clusters of flies complete the effect. When a fly lands on the flower thinking it is joining other flies for a meal, it can't hold on to the slippery surface and slides off into a large pouch formed by the flower's lower petal. Once in the pouch, the fly can only escape by crawling up a narrow tunnel, rubbing off any pollen it received from other flowers and picking up a new load, while it is in the process of leaving.

Coryanthes speciosa, the bucket orchid, in the early morning produces a delightful fragrance that attracts bees. The part of the flower that produces this fragrance is slippery and positioned above glands that secrete fluid into the bucket. Because the flower is so slippery, the bee slides into the bucket, wetting its wings and preventing flight. After frantic struggling, the bee finds a way out through a narrow tunnel at one end of the bucket. It clambers up through this tunnel and emerges with pollinia stuck to its body. The next day the bee, recovered from its ordeal but still carrying its payload of pollen, becomes overwhelmed by the fragrance of another bucket orchid. This time some of the pollen rubs off while the bee is escaping through the tunnel and pollinates the flower.

FLOWER STRUCTURES: Orchids accomplish their reproductive feats with variations on a basic theme of three petals and three sepals. In cattleyas, these parts are easily identified. The two uppermost petals are brightly colored; the highly modified lower petal is a large, ruffled labellum (Latin for lip). The sepals stick out between and behind the petals like the points of a three-pointed star.

The labellum is often the largest and most colorful part of an orchid flower. It can take many different forms. In slipper orchids, the labellum forms a slipper-shaped pouch. In many oncidium flowers, it fans out like a skirt, inspiring the name "dancing dolls."

Orchids share this combination of three petals and three sepals with lilies. Orchids, however, are distinguished from other flowers by the column, an intricate structure formed by the fused male and female reproductive parts—the stamen and pistil. Although the stamen and pistil are very close together on the column, self-pollination is prevented by a divider called the rostellum. Self-pollination may also be prevented by a variety of other mechanisms, most of which are designed to attach pollen to an insect after it has passed the pistil and is on its way out of the flower.

The column can be the most interesting part of an orchid flower. Some columns look like the faces of humans, insects, or birds; others resemble African masks. They may bear wings or wear caps, goggles, or ruffled bonnets. The column of the tiger orchid (*Odontoglossum grande*) resembles a doll.

POLLINATION—TRAPS AND TRIGGERS: Orchid pollen, usually massed into clumps called pollinia, is different from the fluffy powder produced by most other insect-pollinated plants. In cattleyas, an insect (usually a bee) is lured under the column by a supply of nectar or by the flower's enticing fragrance. On its way out, the bee's back becomes coated with a sticky adhesive that catches and attaches one or more of the pollinia. The pollinia in a catasetum orchid are spring-loaded. When a bee bumps the trigger, the pollinia are ejected from the flower onto the insect's body, where they stick tightly. If you trigger the flower with the tip of a pencil held out of the line of fire, the pollinia can shoot several feet.

ABUNDANT FLOWERS: Orchid flowers are borne on inflorescences known as spikes, either singly or in clusters, which may have from five to 25 or more flowers. The flowers at the base of a spike will often open before those at the tip. But because the flowers last a long time, many plants will dazzle you by displaying nearly all of their flowers for most of the time the plant is in bloom.

Pathiopedilums attract flies with a foul odor and fuzzy black warts on their petals. Then it traps them in its pouch. As the fly searches for an exit, it pollinates the flower.

FLORAL LONGEVITY

Orchid flowers look durable, and they are. Waxy paphiopedilum blossoms last for more than a month. Their spikes can linger for three months. The spikes of phalaenopsis, oncidium, and a few other orchids may send out side branches with new buds after the main flowers on the spike have faded. In this way, a plant may remain in bloom for six to eight months. A floriferous phalaenopsis may even have two blooming cycles in one year. Orchids don't display their flowers for such long periods simply for our delight. They are holding out for insects to pollinate them. Once fertilized, orchid flowers quickly fade, and the plant turns its energy to making seed. Unless an appropriate fly or bee happens into your home, or you pollinate the flowers yourself, your plants will remain in bloom until the flowers die.

With blossoms mimicking a swarm of bees, some oncidiums trick bees into a "fight," and thus, ensure pollination.

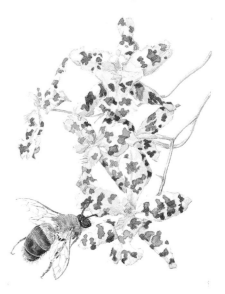

ORCHID BREEDING

This specimen of Dendrobium Violet Yamaji 'Jill's Purple Passion' earned a Certificate of Cultural Merit (CCM/AOS).

SOWING SEEDS

Orchid seeds are sown on nutrient-enriched, sterile agar in a sterilized glass flask. The materials can be purchased from orchid suppliers (see page 92), or you can engage the services of an orchid specialist to do the flasking phase.

A fluorescent-light garden is often the ideal place for starting orchid seeds. After four to six months, there will be tiny seedlings (technically "protocorms") in the flask, and after eight to 18 months they can be separated, graded, and put back into the flasks to grow for about two years. At this point, the seedlings will be ready to transplant about an inch apart into seedling grade orchid bark in community pots, then after a year or so, into individual pots. The first flowers occur in three to seven years.

Because orchid seeds are never sold off the racks the way other flower seeds are, the idea of growing them from scratch rarely occurs, much less the thought of cross-pollinating and creating new plants. The good news is that ever-increasing numbers of amateur orchid growers are dabbling in breeding. In order to do this, you must master the techniques for starting the infinitesimally small seeds.

Step one of breeding is to have in bloom at the same time potential pollen (male) and seed (female) parents that are genetically compatible. Typically, to be compatible, the parents will be of the same genus or at least from the same tribe, if not subtribe.

Often the stronger of the two plants will be selected to play the female role. Take pollen from the flower selected as the male. It will be found in two golden masses on the column, which are called pollinia. Dip tweezers or a sharpened stick under the anther, which holds the pollinia, and the pollinia will stick to it. Set the pollen aside while you remove the pollen from the flower of the selected female parent. Now press pollen from the male parent onto the stigma of the female, which is on the underside of the column.

After pollination, the flower will soon fade and the ovaries, which form the seed capsule (pod) will begin to swell. After five to nine months the seeds will be ripe. Watch for splitting as well as yellowing of the capsule itself.

HYBRIDS

The orchid's wide-ranging sexual compatibility gives breeders the freedom to produce stunning new orchids by crossing plants that are only remotely related. The offspring of these crosses are called hybrids.

When two orchid species in the same genus are crossed, the resulting hybrid seedlings are given a name. Orchid breeders name their hybrids after family members, spouses, mountains, rivers—almost anything goes as long as it doesn't sound like Latin. (Many old hybrid names sounded like Latin, but in 1959 the taxonomists changed the rules to prohibit Latinized hybrid names because it was hard to tell the species from the hybrids.) To be made official, a hybrid name must be registered with the Royal Horticultural Society (RHS), which lists it in *Sander's Complete List of Orchid Hybrids*. Once a hybrid has an official name, all plants resulting from a cross between those parents carry that name, even if subsequent crosses produce very different-looking results, which they often do.

INTERGENERIC HYBRIDS: Orchid breeders have great fun crossing orchids of different genera. This is remarkable genetics; few plants other than orchids can be interbred in this way to create new genera.

An intergeneric hybrid may be named in one of two ways. In the simplest way, the hybrid name is formed by combining the two genus names, as in *Miltassia* from *Miltonia* and

Orchid pollen is contained in waxy yellow masses or balls called pollinia which occur on the column of the flower. Pollinia are naturally sticky.

Use tweezers or a sharpened stick to remove the pollen from the flower of the orchid plant selected to be the male parent of the cross.

Remove the pollinia from the flower selected to be the seed (female) parent. Then place on its stigma the pollen from the male.

Brassia. These names make it easy to remember the parents of the hybrid. The hybrid of *Miltonia spectabilis* and *Brassia verrucosa*, for example, is called *Miltassia* Charles M. Fitch. It has a popular cultivar, 'Dark Monarch' (see "An Orchid Family Tree," page 55).

When a bigeneric hybrid (a hybrid of two genera) is crossed with a plant in yet another genus, the three names may be lumped together as in *Sophrolaeliocattleya*, the cross of *Sophronitis*, *Laelia*, and *Cattleya*. When the names of the genera don't flow smoothly together, taxonomists avoid tongue twisters by giving the hybrid an entirely new name ending with *ara*. For example, the hybrid *Cochlioda* × *Miltonia* × *Odontoglossum* was named *Vuylstekeara* to honor C. Vuylsteke, a Belgian orchid breeder. Another delightful hybrid, *Potinara*, results from crossing *Brassavola*, *Laelia*, *Cattleya*, and *Sophronitis*.

With so many species, varieties, hybrids, and cultivars around, it is necessary to distinguish outstanding orchids from those that are merely pretty. The international awards system codified by the American Orchid Society in 1949 sets the standards.

When evaluating an orchid, judges compare it with all others of the same type that they have seen. To make such comparisons, an orchid judge goes through at least six years of training—three years as a student judge and three years on probation.

CRITERIA FOR JUDGING ORCHIDS

In most cases, orchids are judged solely on the basis of their flowers. Judges consider color, size, shape, and substance (thickness) as well as the way the flowers are borne on the stems. The sharpness and clarity of any stripes, spots, or other markings on petals are also evaluated.

The flowers are evaluated on a 100-point scale. To be considered for an award, an orchid must pass an initial screening. If the judges feel the orchid has a chance of receiving an award, it is entered in formal judging. The best award is the First Class Certificate (FCC/AOS). For this, the orchid must be awarded 90 points or more.

The Award of Merit (AM/AOS) is the next-best award, and is by no means easy to attain. For an Award of Merit, the plant must receive between 80 and 89 points. A plant bearing the letters AM/AOS after its name will have exceptionally beautiful flowers.

The third award is the Highly Commended Certificate (HCC/AOS). An HCC/AOS plant, having received between 75 and 79 points, is still an excellent orchid.

Species orchids may be eligible for two additional awards. The Certificate of Botanical Recognition (CBR/AOS) is awarded to cultivars of species or natural hybrids deemed worthy of recognition for their rarity, novelty, or educational value. The Certificate of Horticultural Merit (CHM/AOS) is given to well-grown species considered particularly interesting from a horticultural standpoint.

And finally, you don't have to breed a new hybrid or collect a new species to receive an AOS award. The Certificate of Cultural Merit (CCM/AOS) is awarded to the grower of an outstanding specimen plant that has enjoyed perfect growing conditions. For this category, the whole plant is judged, not just the flowers. To have your efforts rewarded with a CCM/AOS is a notable achievement.

WHAT KIND OF ORCHID IS THAT?

Dendrobium chrysotoxum *has sweetly scented flowers 2 to 3 inches across. The* **species is widely distributed throughout Asia and is easy to grow.**

Epidendrum ibaguense *(formerly known as* E. radicans*) is widely distributed in Central America.*

Orchids are named under the same international system that governs the naming of all other plants. But orchids aren't exactly like other plants. The orchid family is incredibly large and orchid species interbreed so easily that it is often difficult to tell where one species stops and the next begins. It is the taxonomists' challenge to organize the myriad forms and colors of orchids into neat—and discrete—categories.

The complexity of these categories is reflected in the fine distinctions made among apparently similar plants and hybrids that have elaborate family trees. However, the basic principles are those followed in the naming of any plant. Few people can rattle off the various rules and exceptions of orchid naming, but for any grower, even a general notion of the system will contribute to the enjoyment to be derived from this remarkably diverse family of plants.

HOW ORCHIDS ARE NAMED

To understand how an orchid gets its name, it is best to start at the top, with the orchid family (*Orchidaceae*). For most plants, the next major category used below family is the genus (or

genera if you are speaking of more than one). Because the orchid family is so large, botanists use intermediate categories between the family and genus called tribe and subtribe, categories that can be helpful because they show how the plants in the different genera are related.

The genus *Miltonia*, for example, is in the subtribe *Oncidiinae*. This subtribe also includes the genera *Oncidium, Odontoglossum,* and *Brassia*, all of which have similar characteristics and hybridize easily.

The genus name, such as *Miltonia* or *Brassia*, is an essential part of an orchid's identification. To show that it is a genus name, the word is printed in italics and the first letter is capitalized.

Again for most plants, a genus is divided into species, the basic units of classification in both the plant and animal kingdoms. Species names are printed in italics but are not capitalized. The genus *Miltonia*, for example, contains the species *spectabilis*. An easy way to remember how genus and species names are related is to look at the first few letters of both words. Genus is general; species is specific. The plants in a given species are all quite similar, but you will still find differences in flower size, shape, and color, as well as in the leaves, stems, and pseudobulbs.

Sometimes certain plants in a species share a characteristic that makes them different from others in the species, but not quite different enough to justify a new species name. If such a group is found in nature, it is called a variety. Variety names are often preceded by the abbreviation var. and are printed in lowercase italics. *Miltonia spectabilis* var. *moreliana*, for example, has rose rather than white flower petals, but aside from this

This stunning hybrid moth orchid is from a cross of **Phalaenopsis Abendrot × Ida Fukumura.**

Cattleya Guatemalensis represents a fairly complex hybrid gained through a cross with C. bowringiana. Hybrid orchids with genes from C. bowringiana bloom profusely.

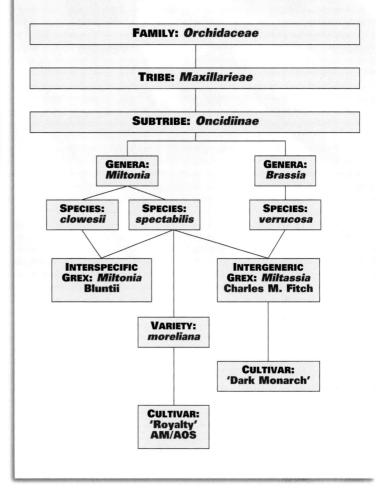

difference in color it is virtually identical to the white-petaled forms of *Miltonia spectabilis*.

Variety names are used primarily by botanists, who study populations of wild plants. In horticulture—the study of cultivated plants—the term "cultivar" is used more frequently. Cultivars are plants selected for their desirable features and propagated in ways that perpetuate those features. A cultivar may be selected from a species, hybrid, or a variety. It may be propagated by division, offshoots, mericloning, or by any other asexual method that produces offspring similar to the parent plant. Cultivar names are printed in roman letters. The first letter is capitalized, and the entire name is enclosed in single quotes. For example, it turns out that one of the prettiest forms of *Miltonia spectabilis* var. *moreliana* has been widely cultivated and awarded. This clone, named 'Royalty', is a cultivar of a variety. It takes its place at the bottom of the family tree.

ORCHIDS WITH MORE THAN ONE NAME: Unfortunately, everyone doesn't always use the same names for orchids. Over the years, taxonomists have tried and discarded several schemes for organizing orchids along evolutionary lines. The goal—a classification system that shows how plants are related—is worthwhile, but becomes difficult to attain when many names must be changed to reflect a new botanical discovery.

To return to the family tree, the name of the cross between *Miltonia spectabilis* and *Miltonia clowesii* is *Miltonia* Bluntii (you can tell from the word's Latin ending that this is an old hybrid, named before the rules prohibited Latinized hybrid names). *Miltonia* Bluntii is a primary hybrid—also known as an interspecific grex—produced when one species is crossed with another species. Primary hybrids are not as common as more

complex hybrids, which are produced when a hybrid is crossed with a species or another hybrid. Now that the value of species orchids is becoming widely recognized (see "Endangered Orchids," page 18), primary hybrids are coming back into vogue.

COMMON NAMES: Common orchid names are as confusing and misleading as the common names of other plants. Although easier to pronounce, the words rarely point directly to a specific plant and are thus of little value. A single common name often applies to several species—species that have nothing else in common. For example, there seems to be at least one spider orchid on every continent, and new ones are probably dubbed every day. Better simply to call them all orchids, a very general but at least correct name. At any rate, most orchid species don't have common names. The genus name is often used informally as the common name. In this book, for example, when the genus *Cattleya* is discussed, the word is treated as a common name, as in "cattleyas are easy to grow" or "phalaenopsis can be confidence builders."

ORCHID GALLERY

Within this gallery, you will find some of the best orchids for growing in windows, light gardens, greenhouses, and outdoors. To help you choose wisely, each orchid has been rated as to whether it is suitable for a beginner, intermediate, or advanced grower. The rating depends on the adaptability of the orchid, that is, how easily it will forgive underwatering or overwatering, too much or too little light, and temperatures that vary from the ideal. The somewhat exacting seasonal treatments required by a few of the orchids (such as the late fall and winter drying-out required by deciduous dendrobiums) may earn them a rating of "advanced."

The entries in this guide are organized alphabetically by genus. Most genera contain many more species. Occasionally, as in the case of Cattleya labiata, the species is now rarely grown but its hybrid progeny are found in collections all over the world. Most of the orchids offered for sale are hybrids. Every year new hybrids are introduced. The last part of each genus description highlights the most recent work of the orchid breeders.

Each orchid entry begins with a quick, care-at-a-glance section that includes a pronunciation guide for the botanical name. The next line identifies the plants in the genus as sympodial or monopodial. This information (see pages 20 to 21) gives an overall impression of how the plants grow and is helpful when it's time to divide and repot.

The orchid's preferences for light and temperature—two of the most critical factors—are shown next. Light is described as high, medium, or low (see "Ideal Light Ranges," page 7). Temperature requirements are given as cool, intermediate, or warm—terms that are defined in degrees on pages 12 and 13. The flowering seasons are listed next. By considering natural bloom time in your orchid selection, you can assemble a collection that flowers all year.

The last care-at-a-glance line gives a care rating: beginner, intermediate, or advanced, assuming basic light, temperature, and water requirements can be met. The rest of the entry describes the genus in more detail, what the species in the genus have in common and what their importance is in the overall scheme of orchid plants.

Brassavola
bra-SAH-vo-la

- Sympodial
- Light: Medium to high
- Temperature: Warm to intermediate
- Flowering: Summer to fall
- Care: Beginner

The genus *Brassavola* is composed of Latin American epiphytes, closely related to plants in the genera *Cattleya* and *Laelia*. Their star-shaped flowers are deliciously fragrant at night, but the scent becomes almost imperceptible shortly after daybreak. Easily grown with cattleyas and laelias, brassavolas demand plenty of light but tolerate humidity as low as 40 percent. Propagate plants by division after flowering.

SPECIES

■ ***BRASSAVOLA CUCCULATA:*** This orchid has longer (8 to 18 inches), narrower leaves than the more commonly grown *B. nodosa*. Carl von Linné first described it in 1763 as *Epidendrum cucullatum*. When another orchid fancier introduced the genus *Brassavola* in 1813, he made *cucculata* the type for the species. Plants occur from Mexico to northern South America and into the West Indies. The orchid's decorative, spidery, nocturnally fragrant flowers bloom from summer into winter. Along with its robust growth, this has made *B. cucculata* popular with breeders. The sepals and petals are pale yellow ("straw") to white on the inner

Brassolaelia *Yellow Bird 'Jean' is from a cross of* Bl. *Richard Mueller* × Brassavola nodosa.

surface, attractively blushed with reddish brown on the outside, or reverses.

■ ***B. DIGBYANA:*** Introduced into cultivation from Honduras and first brought into flower in England in 1845 by Edward St. Vincent Digby, botanist John Lindley named the species in Digby's honor the following year and published it under the name *Brassavola digbyana*. Subsequently it was moved for a time to the genus *Laelia*, until 1918, when Rudolf Schlecter determined that

Brassolaelia *Richard Mueller flowers suggest the airy, spidery ones of its parent* Brassavola nodosa. *Color and habit are from* Laelia milleri *parent.*

Brassolaeliocattleya *Toshie Aoki 'Pizazz' inherits vigor from the brassavola parent, flower size and color from laelia and cattleya genes.*

Brassolaeliocattleya *Golden Liewellyn is exceptional for its large, ruffled lip and for the picotee edging of the large, rounded petals.*

it belonged in a separate though closely related genus and henceforth should be known as *Rhyncholaelia digbyana*. For orchid hybrid registration purposes it has continued to be referred to as a brassavola, and so that name is the one commonly used.

Whatever the name, it is a popular parent in crosses with cattleya and laelia, giving the large flower size and prized, fringed lip to many cattleya hybrids. It is also worth growing in its own right for its 4- to 6-inch greenish white flowers with lacy labellum and lemony fragrance. The narrow, silvery leaves are succulent and 8 to 10 inches long.

Respect its rest period—water lightly and withhold fertilizer for several months after flowering. Native from Mexico to Guatemala, it needs warmth and high light and often does better on a bark mount instead of in a pot—to assure that the roots are never soggy.

■ **B. NODOSA:** Called the "lady of the night" in Latin America for its exquisite evening perfume, *B. nodosa's* 3-inch flowers may be white with tiny purple dots on the lip, greenish-white, or cream. The foliage is upright and varies in height from a compact 4 inches to 12 inches. Unlike *B. digbyana*, *B. nodosa* does not need a dry rest period—it usually grows and flowers year round. It is native from Mexico through Central America

to Peru and Venezuela; also found in the West Indies.

■ **B. TUBERCULATA (B. PERRINII):** Collected in Brazil, this large epiphyte or lithophyte was first brought into flower near Liverpool, England, in 1828. The spidery, airy, nocturnally fragrant flowers are palest yellow to lime and they appear in great numbers on an established plant, which is often seen on a slab of cork or other type mount. The elliptically shaped lip is white and may be flushed green in the throat. The flowers themselves never open fully and the sepals in some plants have blood-red spotting. While current authorities list this brassavola as the species *tuberculata*, it has in fairly recent times been known as *B. perrinii*, with cultivar 'Emily' earning a CCM/AOS.

HYBRIDS

■ **BRASSAVOLA DAVID SANDER:** An early hybrid of *B. digbyana* and *B. cucullata*, this orchid has narrow, pinkish white petals and a perfectly fringed lip. It has pencil-sized, shiny leaves.

Brassavolas are crossed with cattleyas to form brassocattleyas, or with cattleyas and laelias to form brassolaeliocattleyas.

BRASSAVOLA CULTIVARS AND HYBRIDS

Brassavola digbyana 'Dragonstone' HCC/AOS

B. nodosa 'Mendenhall' AM/AOS

B. nodosa 'Orchidglade'

B. David Sander

B. perrinii 'Emily' CCM/AOS

Brassocattleya Binosa (*Brassavola nodosa* × *Cattleya bicolor*)

Brassolaelia Citron Star (*Brassavola nodosa* × *Laelia gloedeniana*)

Brassolaeliocattleya (*Brassavola* × *Laelia* × *Cattleya*) Cornerstone '4th of July' AM/AOS

Blc. Everything Nice 'Exquisite' AM/AOS

Blc. Goldenzelle 'Lemon Chiffon' AM/AOS

TIPS FOR SUCCESS

Use growing medium A (see "Recipes for Favorite Mixes," page 26) in a pot with drain holes or in a basket. Brassavola species can also be grown as bark mounts, particularly in tropical and subtropical climates where they can be hung outdoors most of the year. The plants will live indefinitely in low light; however, in order to thrive and bloom regularly, they need strong light and good air movement.

The species can be brought to bloom twice or more yearly by alternating periods of freely watering and fertilizing with periods of maintaining plants on the dry side and withholding fertilizer. For this reason, they are considered worthwhile plants for the indoor gardener who must make every inch of growing space count.

Brassavolas accept a wide range of temperatures, from cool to warm and can bloom successfully in window or fluorescent light. Their tolerance for relatively low humidity—to around 40 percent—makes them choice houseplants and noteworthy confidence builders.

Brassavola nodosa *or "lady of the night" is one of the species orchids that has remained popular in cultivation. It is quite often recommended as an ideal beginner's orchid for growing as a houseplant.*

Brassia
BRASS-ee-ah

- ■ Sympodial
- ■ Light: Medium
- ■ Temperature: Intermediate
- ■ Flowering: Late spring to early summer
- ■ Care: Beginner

Orchids in the genus *Brassia* are among the many orchids commonly called spider orchids. In this case, the name is appropriately descriptive. The slender, pointed sepals and petals of the flowers could resemble spider legs, and the lip is shaped much like a spider's body. Fortunately, spiders in the normal course of things don't grow as large as these gargantuan flowers. The extraordinary blossoms of some forms can stretch more than 16 inches from top to bottom.

Brassias don't come in a wide variety of colors, but their hues are appealing and, to some collectors, they are irresistible. Most are gold to green, speckled or banded with brown, purple, or maroon. Almost all of the 30 species have fragrant flowers. Well-grown plants may bear literally hundreds of blossoms, perfectly spaced on gently arching spikes. Each large, flattened pseudobulb bears two or three long, leathery leaves. Most plants grow to about 2 feet tall, though some may reach 3 feet.

Brassias can be treated like cattleyas, but they should not be allowed to dry out completely when they are actively growing. Propagate brassias by dividing the pseudobulbs after flowering.

Brassia maculata *(West Indies and Central America) has a long bloom season.*

SPECIES

■ **BRASSIA GIREOUDIANA:** The large, flattened pseudobulbs and leathery leaves of this species are typical of the genus. The flowers are abundantly fragrant and measure up to 12 inches from top to bottom. The sepals and petals are greenish-yellow, blotched near their bases with shiny black or brown markings. The large, pale yellow lip spreads widely at the tip. It has a few brown spots near the center. The exceptionally large, well-shaped flowers of *Brs. gireoudiana* 'Town Hill'

Brassia *Sunrise Glow 'Allison' is from a cross of* Brs. gireoudiana × Brs. *Sunset Gold. Brassia hybrids have exceptional vigor.*

Wingfieldara *Casseta 'Everglades' is from a cross of* Brassia Rex × Wfga. Browning Island. (Wfga. = Aspasia × Brassia × Odontoglossum.)

A cross of Brassia × Oncidium Honolulu 'Vashon' produced this eye-catching flower on a plant having exceptional vigor.

earned it an AM/AOS. *Brs. gireoudiana* flowers in late spring to summer. It is native to Costa Rica and Panama.

■ **BRS. MACULATA:** This species is similar to *Brs. gireoudiana*, except that the flowers are smaller (from 5 to 8 inches long) and are spotted with purple. They also last a very long time, up to a month and a half. The cultivar *Brs. maculata* 'Monte Vista' received an HCC/AOS. *Brs. maculata* blooms at any time between fall and spring and sometimes blooms twice a year. It is found in Guatemala, Honduras, Venezuela, Cuba, and Jamaica.

HYBRIDS

Crosses between brassia species have produced vigorous, adaptable hybrids such as Edvah Loo (*Brs. longissima* × *Brs. gireoudiana*) and Rex (*Brs. gireoudiana* × *Brs. verrucosa*). Both have large fragrant flowers with brown markings.

Orchid breeders often "add a little brassia" to other genera to increase flower size and plant vigor. Crosses of brassias with oncidiums produce what is known as the *Brassidium*, a new genus of plants with large numbers of big yellow flowers variously marked with brown.

Miltonias are crossed with brassias to form a new orchid known as a *Miltassia* that is favored for its generous production of star-shaped flowers with ruffled lips. Miltassias are easy, flowering and growing in a wide range of temperatures and forgiving the beginner's sometimes unsteady green thumb.

One of the best known miltassias is Charles M. Fitch 'Amethyst', named to honor photographer, horticulturist, orchid breeder, and educator Charles Marden Fitch. Fitch has made a particularly noteworthy contribution of beautiful orchid photography for publication by the American Orchid Society. It is appropriate that an exceptional orchid honor an exceptional person.

Combinations of three genera— *Brassia*, *Oncidium*, and *Miltonia*— result in the *Aliceara* hybrids. These plants bear dozens of enormous flowers in combinations of rich gold and maroon, yellow and chocolate, orange and yellow, and green and white. Some recent introductions include *Aliceara* Kolan Beauty (*Aliceara* Pathfinder × *Oncidium gravesianum*), *Alcra.* Iro Otoko (*Alcra.* Dorothy Oka × *Miltonia* Castanea), and *Alcra.* Millenium Falcon (*Brassidium* Gilded Urchin × *Miltonia* Belle Glade).

TIPS FOR SUCCESS

Brassias will grow well in any standard, all-purpose orchid bark mix or Growing Medium A (see "Recipes for Favorite Mixes," page 26). Young plants may benefit from being transplanted yearly to a size or two larger pot each time. After the first flowering, repotting may not be needed except every two years (before the growing medium begins to decompose). If growing outdoors, brassias require a little less light than cattleyas. Indoors, they are suited to a half-sunny window, such as one receiving direct sun from the east or south, perhaps a little more shade if from the hot, western sun. Under lights, brassias can be accommodated under banks of four to six 40- or 74-watt tubes burned 16 hours out of every 24. Be sure that brassias do not dry out severely between waterings. When grown with a steady hand, they are capable of having beautiful foliage that rises above smooth, green pseudobulbs. The effect can be enhanced by cleaning the leaves and pseudobulbs of any spray or hard water residue by using fresh lemon juice. This gives them a natural, attractive sheen.

BRASSIA CULTIVARS AND HYBRIDS

Brassia gireoudiana 'Town Hill' AM/AOS

Brs. maculata 'Monte Vista' HCC/AOS

Brs. Edvah Loo (*Brs. longissima* × *Brs. gireoudiana*) 'Mark Daniel' HCC/AOS

Brs. Memoria Fritz Boedeker 'Witch Doctor'

Brs. longissima 'Olivia'

Brs. Rex (*Brs. gireoudiana* × *Brs. verrucosa*)

Brs. Rex 'Christine' AM/AOS

Brs. Rex 'Tahoma' AM/AOS

Brs. Spiders Revenge

Brs. verrucosa 'Horich'

Brassidium Seminole Hideway (*Oncidium* Colon × *Brassia arcuigera*)

Introduced from Jamaica, Brassia maculata was first flowered in cultivation at the Royal Botanic Gardens, Kew in 1813. It is a large, robust epiphyte, that occasionally grows as a lithophyte. It is easy to grow and useful in breeding work to create hybrids such as this.

Cattleya
KAT-lee-ah

- ■ Sympodial
- ■ Light: Medium to high
- ■ Temperature: Intermediate to warm
- ■ Flowering: Variable
- ■ Care: Beginner

Cattleya loddigesii, *from Brazil, flowers in summer and fall and often in other seasons.*

When most people think of an orchid, they think of a cattleya, the prom-night corsage. Important in orchid history, the genus was named after William Cattley, the English horticulturist who first brought these beautiful plants into flower outside of their native habitat. Cattley didn't intend to discover a genus of highly evolved flowering plants. He was devoting his efforts to the lowly mosses and lichens shipped to him from South America by a plant explorer named Swainson. In preparing his shipments, Swainson used the cattleya plant's stiff leathery leaves and pseudobulbs to reinforce the bundles of mosses. Cattley's curiosity was piqued by the odd plants, so he potted them up. When the plants started blooming in 1824, Cattley showed them to John Lindley, a famous botanist. Lindley recognized that these gorgeous flowers were new to science, and named the genus *Cattleya* and the species *labiata,* in reference to the flower's impressive lip. Word of the discovery spread quickly, inciting an orchid mania. To this day, the cattleya reigns as queen of the orchids.

Cattleyas are divided into two groups according to the number of leaves arising from the pseudobulbs: unifoliate and bifoliate.

Unifoliate cattleyas have a single leaf on each pseudobulb, and grow between 1 and 2 feet tall. The flowers, borne one to five per stem, are between 2 and 7 inches across. Hybrid flowers may be even larger. Their large, ruffled lip is often marked with colorful patterns.

Unifoliates may also be called labiates in reference to *Cattleya labiata,* the most important species in the group. Although other unifoliates were once commonly grown, they are now expensive and difficult to obtain, having been largely supplanted by hybrids.

Cattleya *Portia produces several medium-sized flowers in each inflorescence. They last about two weeks and give off a light scent.*

Laeliocattleya *Dinard 'Blue Heaven' is one of the bluer orchids in the cattleya tribe. It is fall-blooming, a cross of St. Gothard × C. Dinah.*

Art shades, flame colors, and flowers with splash marks can be found among modern cattleya hybrids, most involving other genera.

Species in the bifoliate group of cattleyas have two (or sometimes three) leaves atop long, slender pseudobulbs. Bifoliates range from 15 inches to 5 feet tall. The flowers, which are generally thicker and smaller than those of the unifoliates, are borne 10 to 25 per spike and usually last longer than those of the unifoliates.

SPECIES

Species cattleyas have largely given way to hybrids, but there are several superior species forms still available.

■ **CATTLEYA AURANTIACA:** This bifoliate grows to 1 foot tall. The flowers are thick, fragrant, bright orange or orange-red, and 1 inch across. It blooms from summer to fall. Commonly used in breeding, C. *aurantiaca* is an ancestor of many of the orange to red hybrids. It occurs in Mexico, Guatemala, El Salvador, Honduras, and Nicaragua.

■ **C. BICOLOR:** The shoots of this bifoliate may reach 4 feet. Its flowers are fragrant, and spread up to 4 inches across. The sepals and petals are golden green with a coppery tinge and the narrow lip is a brilliant purplish red. The plant flowers in the fall and may bloom again in spring. It is found in Brazil.

TIPS FOR SUCCESS

Cattleyas are among the easiest orchids to grow. Their thick pseudobulbs enable them to withstand periods of drought, forgiving the forgetful gardener. Attentive gardeners may need to be careful to not overwater. The growing medium needs to dry out almost completely—but not quite—between waterings. (See pages 32–33 for tips on how to check the moisture content of the growing medium and how to water properly.) Cattleyas growing in fir bark generally need to be watered about once a week when they are in active growth. After flowering, cattleyas enter a resting phase lasting a month or two. During this time of semidormancy, increase the intervals between waterings and don't fertilize at all.

Cattleya flowers last about two weeks on the plant. Cut flowers last about a week. To make them last as long as possible, don't cut the flowers until they have fully expanded and thickened—about three to five days after they open. Although they may be richly fragrant on the plant, the flowers lose their fragrance when cut. Fingers touching the flowers will prematurely age the petals.

■ **C. GUTTATA:** Usually about 3 feet tall, vigorous forms of this bifoliate may grow to 5 feet. The fragrant yellow-green flowers are marked with purple. The lip is usually magenta, and may have white lobes. It flowers from late fall to winter. C. *guttata* is often used in hybridization. It is native to Brazil.

■ **C. LABIATA:** This unifoliate grows 2 feet tall. Its rosy flowers have excellent proportions and a fine texture. The large, ruffled lip— for which the species is named—is deep rose with dark lines leading to a pair of yellow spots in the throat. The flowers are fragrant and long lasting. The plants bloom in fall in response to shorter days. A lamp left on in the evening during fall can prevent flowering. It is native to Brazil.

■ **C. SKINNERI:** This bifoliate is about 2 feet tall. Its rose, purple, or white flowers are about 3 inches across with a glittery texture and a faint fragrance. The plant has an excellent habit and makes many new growths every year. It flowers from late winter to spring. This species may be found in Mexico, Guatemala, Honduras, Costa Rica, Colombia, Venezuela, and Bolivia.

CATTLEYA CULTIVARS AND HYBRIDS

Cattleya aurantiaca
  'Citronella'
  HCC/AOS
C. *dowiana*
  'Meadowlark'
C. × *guatemalensis*
  'Marge Soule'
  HCC/AOS
C. *skinneri* var. *alba*
  'Yolanda Cuesta'
  FCC/AOS
Brassolaeliocattleya
  Clyde's Melody
  'Orchidglade'
  AM/AOS
Otaara (*Brassavola* ×
  Broughtonia ×
  Cattleya × *Laelia*)
  Jane Fumiye
  'Hawaii' AM/AOS
Potinara Heavenly
  Jewel 'Puanani'
  AM/AOS
Sophrolaeliocattleya
  Jewel Box
  'Scheherazade'
  CCM/AOS

HYBRIDS

Thousands of cattleya hybrids have been produced. Most involve crosses with plants in other genera, for example: brassolaeliocattleya (brassavola × laelia × cattleya), epicattleya (epidendrum × cattleya), laeliocattleya (laelia × cattleya), potinara (brassavola × cattleya × laelia × sophronitis), and sophrolaeliocattleya (sophronitis × laelia × cattleya).

The range of colors, patterns, and fragrances found in hybrids is astounding. Flowers in rose, pink, and lavender may have lips of vivid chartreuse, with yellow markings in the throat. Yellow flowers may be pure gold or tinged with green and have red markings on their lips. The green forms with yellow- or red-marked lips often have lemony fragrances. Whites and semialbas usually have contrasting lips marked with red, purple, or yellow.

Cattleya amethystoglossa is from Brazil. The spotted flowers appear in clusters (three to eight) on tall plants, to 3 feet. Discovered in 1862, it blooms midsummer.

Cymbidium
sim-BID-ee-um

- ■ Sympodial
- ■ Light: Standards (bright); miniatures (medium to bright)
- ■ Temperature: Standards (cool); miniatures (cool to intermediate)
- ■ Flowering: Variable; peak in early spring
- ■ Care: Beginner

Substantial, waxy, long-lasting cymbidium flowers are as common in flower shops as cattleya. Cymbidium's flower colors, which include all but blue, are often combined in lovely patterns. Imagine, for example, a pistachio-green flower with a scarlet-and-white lip. Individual flowers are popular for corsages or arrangements and, when left on the plant, last between eight and 10 weeks.

Hardly anyone grows species cymbidiums anymore. Years of intense breeding have given us hybrids that outshine the species in flower form, extraordinary colors, and longevity. Cymbidium hybrids are also usually easier to grow, tolerating broader ranges of temperature and blooming more freely.

Cymbidium *Golden Elf* is a superb miniature with fragrant flowers in summer or fall.

HYBRIDS

Cymbidium hybrids fall into two main groups, standards and miniatures. Standard cymbidiums bear flowers between 3 and 5 inches across and grow up to 3 feet tall. They require bright sunlight and very cool night temperatures. Along the California coast, where these requirements are easily satisfied, standard cymbidiums are considered low-maintenance outdoor plants. In other areas, standard cymbidiums are considered rather difficult, cool-greenhouse plants—officially, that is.

In fact, specimens purchased in bloom as house decorations often are set outdoors in the summer and surprisingly, over much of the continental United States, they adapt and bloom again. The secret is to find a place outdoors where there is good air circulation but protection from strong winds; where the

The delicately rounded flowers of Cymbidium *Hamsey × Musita* show the refinement possible in today's superb, large-flowered hybrids.

Cymbidium *Lucense* has upright spikes of medium-sized flowers in the range of chartreuse and apricot. Flowers last up to two months.

Cymbidium *Magna Charta 'Spring Promise'* is from a cross of Runnymede × Flare and is one of the finest large-flowered hybrids.

sunlight is strong enough to nurture the leaves and pseudobulbs but not to scorch them; and where the hose will be handy to give them water when rainfall is not sufficient to maintain fairly evenly moist conditions. Finally, if cymbidiums are fertilized regularly, left outdoors until the day before frost is predicted—the big chill sets the flower buds—and then brought in to a cozy but not too warm sun porch, they will bear flowers in winter to spring.

The flowers of miniature cymbidiums are between 1 and 3 inches in diameter. Although plants are still too large to be considered true miniature orchids (which are generally less than 1 foot tall), their 1- to 2-foot maximum height makes them more manageable.

Many miniatures will produce flowers in warmer temperatures than will standards, but their high light requirement still makes them greenhouse or outdoor plants. In any event, it is not likely they will prosper as all-year indoor or light-garden plants. However, if miniature cymbidiums can be summered outdoors, they will bloom beautifully indoors through the fall and winter months.

Standards and miniatures are semiterrestrial plants. They need to be kept moist at all times, and are potted in plastic pots in mixes that retain large quantities of water while still allowing adequate aeration. As with other orchids, many mixes are suitable. Some growers use fine fir bark; others pot cymbidiums in a mixture of 20 percent peat moss, 45 percent medium-grade fir bark, and 35 percent redwood chips.

■ **STANDARD HYBRIDS:** Most standard hybrids are produced for the cut-flower trade, where timing is critical. As a result, you can choose plants for bloom in three different seasons. Early hybrids flower before January, midseason hybrids bloom from January to April, and late-season hybrids bloom from April to May. Award-winning hybrids are available for each blooming season.

■ **MINIATURE HYBRIDS:** Miniatures bloom any time from late fall to spring. The newly popular Golden Elf 'Sundust' blooms in summer. A variety of colors is available. Hybrids Showgirl (Sweetheart × Alexanderi), Ivy Fung (Mary Pinchess × Carisona), and Sylvia Miller (Mary Pinchess × Sussex) have received the most awards, but hundreds of other exceptional hybrids are offered. The miniature cymbidium's success guarantees that many more new hybrids will be developed.

CYMBIDIUM CULTIVARS AND HYBRIDS

Cymbidium Ann Miller 'Zuma'
Cym. Gareth 'Round Table'
Cym. Golden Elf 'Sundust' HCC/AOS
Cym. Leodogran 'Villa Park'
Cym. Lipper 'Autumn Splendor'
Cym. Mary Pinchess 'Sparkle'
Cym. Nonna 'Goldilocks' AM/AOS
Cym. Pastoral 'Horizon' HCC/AOS
Cym. Pipeta 'York'
Cym. Sleeping Beauty 'Sarah Jean' HCC/AOS
Cym. Via Ambarino 'Golden Harvest'

TIPS FOR SUCCESS

A most important lesson to learn about cymbidiums is that they are semiterrestrial—partly of the earth—but also of the air. They require a turfy or otherwise humus-rich growing medium that constantly gives the roots air but also nurtures them with a little moisture at all times.

Another important lesson about cymbidiums is their love of sunlight, so much so that the leaves need to appear slightly yellowish green. If they are a nice dark green, then the sunlight is either not strong enough or is not being received for a sufficient duration. Of course, if the leaves actually burn, you've overdone it!

A third lesson about cymbidiums is that the plant needs to be set in a pot of sufficient size to balance the top, probably a clay one—although they do nicely in plastic—and left to establish, until the surface is nearly filled with pseudobulbs. Fertilize faithfully through spring and summer. Top dressing with 14-14-14 timed-release fertilizer pellets can work well, plus 30-10-10 at watering time every other week.

Cymbidium tracyanum, from Burma, southwest China, and Thailand, was first cultivated and described in 1890. Its lavishly colored flowers may appear at any time from autumn to summer.

Dendrobium

den-DROH-bee-um

- ■ Sympodial
- ■ Light: Medium to bright
- ■ Temperature: Warm to cool
- ■ Flowering: Varies depending on species
- ■ Care: Beginner to advanced, depending on species

The genus dendrobium is impossibly large. It contains over 1,000 species, found in a vast area stretching from Korea and Japan through the Malay region and from Indonesia to Australia and New Zealand. New Guinea is especially rich in dendrobiums; it is home to more than 350 species. To help comprehend the complex genus, it is divided into sections, as described in the following paragraphs.

Dendrobium *Delicatum is a floriferous natural hybrid of* Den. kingianum × Den. speciosum.

SECTIONS

■ **CALLISTA:** These are evergreen plants, and most have pseudobulbs. The flower spikes, produced in the spring, are usually pendent, and carry flowers in shades of yellow, white, or lavender. Grow these types under intermediate conditions in summer. In winter, they need cool nights and dry conditions. The youngest pseudobulbs should shrivel slightly during this winter treatment, but water them enough to keep them from wasting away.

Dendrobium *aggregatum*, one of the most popular callista species, is a 3- to 6-inch plant with spindle-shaped pseudobulbs and oblong, leathery leaves. The pendent orange-yellow flowers have a large, rounded lip, and are a little wider than 1 inch in diameter. A single spike may bear up to 30 flowers. Other species in this section include *Den. chrysotoxum*, *densiflorum*, *farmeri*, and *thyrsiflorum*.

■ **SPATULATA:** The species in this section are commonly called "antelope dendrobiums" because the flowers have an upright pair of twisted petals that resemble the horns of an antelope. The plants are evergreen and have no pseudobulbs. They need intermediate conditions throughout the year but tolerate cool winters if kept dry. Spatulata species are easier to grow than some of the others because

G. Ethel Kawamoto *is an antelope type of dendrobium, a complex hybrid of* D. discolor × (taurinum × Tokai).

Dendrobium *Hiang Beauty is of the type familiar to consumers, an orchid that is available in bloom at a reasonable price all year around.*

Dendrobium *White Fairy is typical of the white-flowering hybrids available from local retailers. The spikes stay in bloom for weeks if not months.*

they flower without any special rest. This section includes the species *Den. antennatum, canaliculatum, discolor, gouldii, johannis, lineale, stratiotes, strebloceras*, and *taurinum*.

■ **DENDROBIUM:** These species are deciduous, and most have drooping canes. Flowers are held near the ends of the mature, leafless canes. The plants need medium to bright light and intermediate to cool temperatures in summer. They must have a cool, dry winter to flower—between 40° and 50° F at night, little water, and no fertilizer.

Dendrobium nobile, an upright species, is one of the most popular dendrobiums. Its fragrant flowers are about 3 inches across and usually borne in groups of three. The flower colors are variable, but popular forms have white petals with rose or mauve tips, and a ruffled lip with a deep maroon throat, grading into yellow and white. The edge of the lip may be tinged to match the petals. Other species in this large group include *D. anosmum, chrysanthum, crassinode, falconeri, fimbriatum, findleyanum, friedricksianum, heterocarpum, loddigesii, moniliforme, parishii, primulinum, transparens*, and *wardianum*.

■ **FORMOSAE:** Leaves are evergreen, and the narrow upright pseudobulbs have patches of black hair where the leaves join. Flowers

TIPS FOR SUCCESS

Dendrobiums grow in climates that vary from steamy tropical lowlands to frosty mountain forests, and the flowering habits of the plants are often directly related to seasonal patterns.

In order to flower, some species need cool conditions in the fall, some require a dry spell after the new growths mature, and others need a cool dry spell.

The forms of dendrobium plants vary also. Some are compact, pseudobulbous plants suitable for fluorescent-light gardens; others have thick canes several feet tall.

To make sense of all this, the experts have divided the genus into sections with similar characteristics. Most popular dendrobiums fall into one of the six sections described in the accompanying text.

Dendrobium phalaenopsis will bloom in a light exposure at the low end of the medium range, alongside plants in the genus *Phalaenopsis*. The plants will, however, produce sturdier growths and more flowers if given more light.

Dendrobium nobile plants need to be cool and dry in fall to set the flower buds.

are white, up to 4 inches across, and marked with yellow, orange, green, or violet. Plants in this section require intermediate to cool conditions all year and should dry out slightly in winter. Species include *Den. bellatulum, dearii, draconis, formosum, infundibulum, lowii, lyonii, margaritaceum, sanderae*, and *schuetzii*.

■ **LATOURIA:** The plants are evergreen and have pseudobulbs. The flowers are usually yellow to green. A relatively easy group, these plants grow and flower well in intermediate to cool conditions. No special resting treatments are needed, but keep the plants on the dry side if the temperature drops into the cool range. *Den. atroviolaceum, johnsoniae, macrophyllum*, and *spectabile* are some of the species in this group.

■ **PHALAENANTHE:** These plants may be evergreen or deciduous, depending on the conditions. Their pseudobulbs are tall and thin. The most popular species in this section, *Den. phalaenopsis (syn. bigibbum)*, bears flowers that are similar in many ways to those in the genus phalaenopsis. They have a flattened shape and are arranged on the spike in two parallel rows. The individual flowers last a long time—six to eight weeks—and a plant may remain in bloom for three to four months. Spikes are produced by new and old growths, beginning in early spring. In addition to their floral similarities, *Den. phalaenopsis* require intermediate to warm temperatures all year. Phalaenanthe types need no special treatment, although overwatering will make a plant produce keikis, not flowers. Other species in this section include *Den. affine, bigibbum, dicuphum*, and *williamsianum*.

HYBRIDS

Most dendrobium hybrids are offspring of *Den. nobile* or *Den. phalaenopsis*. Of the *Den. nobile* hybrids, some of the most popular are the Yamamoto crosses, bred by Yamamoto Dendrobiums of Hawaii. These plants are now more commonly grown than the selections of *Den. nobile* species (see list above right).

DENDROBIUM CULTIVARS AND HYBRIDS

Dendrobium densiflorum 'Meredith Ann' CCM/AOS
Den. farmeri 'Jo Ann Lapointe' AM/AOS
Den. lindleyi (syn. *aggregatum*) 'Kiyooko' CCM/AOS
Award-winning Yamamoto Hybrids include:
Utopia 'Messenger'
Sao Paulo 'Memory'
Hagaromo 'Spring Fuji'
Yukidaruma 'King'
Dendrobium phalaenopsis (syn. bigibbum) hybrids:
Anna Bibus
Hickam Deb
Marianne Bates
Ram Misra
Orglade's Orbit
Lady Hamilton

Dendrobium chrysotoxum *is very fragrant and has been treasured by collectors since it was introduced from India into England in 1847.*

Encyclia
en-SIKE-lee-ah

- Sympodial
- Light: Medium
- Temperature: Warm to cool
- Flowering: All seasons, primarily spring to summer
- Care: Beginner

Florida native Encyclia tampensis flowers appear freely in almost any season. They bloom especially heavily in late spring.

ENCYCLIA CULTIVARS AND HYBRIDS

Encyclia cochleata
  'Dancing Lady'
E. tampensis 'Pagoda'
E. Green Glades
  (E. tampensis ×
  E. cordigera)

Also the species and crosses of record:
E. cordigera × self
E. mariae × self
E. odoratissima
E. tampensis × self

Encyclia cordigera, first described in 1815, produces its fragrant flowers in summer. The plant needs intermediate to warm conditions.

Encyclias generally have compact growth habits and freely produce their fragrant flowers while growing under home conditions. The shell-type encyclias, such as *Encyclia cochleata* and *E. fragrans*, are particularly interesting because their "upside-down" flowers look like squid or octopuses. The resemblance ends there; the flowers smell delightful. Encyclias require the same easy-to-provide care as their close relatives, the cattleyas.

SPECIES

ENCYCLIA ADENOCAULA: Strap-like leaves arch from the pseudobulbs; the plant grows between 5 and 8 inches tall. The flower spikes hold many pink to rose-pink blooms with narrow petals. The long pointed lip has dark pink markings and an interesting winged column. It flowers in spring. Native to Mexico.

E. COCHLEATA (EPI. COCHLEATUM): Of all the shell-type encyclias, this one looks the most like an octopus. The plant is about 1 foot high, and it fits neatly under lights. The shell-shaped lip is mostly green with purple and black stripes. The petals and sepals are yellow-green. The plant blooms from fall to spring, often more than once a year. *E. cochleata* is native from Mexico to Venezuela and Cuba.

E. CORDIGERA (EPI. ATROPURPUREUM): This is a heavy plant with conical pseudobulbs and leathery, straplike leaves. It grows up to 2 feet tall. The fragrant flowers have brown to purple petals that curve forward at the tips, and the lip is creamy white with three bright pink splotches. In some forms, the entire lip is rose-red. The flowers appear in spring and summer. Many varieties are available. Native from

Mexico to Peru and Brazil, this species is also found in Cuba.

E. FRAGRANS (EPI. FRAGRANS): This is a stout species with erect growth between 10 and 15 inches tall. It has shell-type, spicily fragrant flowers (hence the species name *fragrans*). The petals and sepals are cream to yellow. The lip is the same color, candy-striped with red. *E. fragrans* blooms from May to June. It is native from Mexico and the West Indies to Ecuador, Peru, and Brazil.

E. TAMPENSIS (EPI. TAMPENSE): This is the "butterfly orchid" of south Florida and the Bahamas. The pseudobulbs cluster to form mats supporting leathery leaves up to 15 inches long. The 1-inch flowers are fragrant and pretty but not particularly spectacular. The sepals and petals are brownish-green to apple-green. The lip is white with a magenta spot. *E. tampensis* usually blooms in spring or summer and is often seen on a bark mount.

TIPS FOR SUCCESS

Because it flowers consecutively for several months on the same spike, *Encyclia cochleata* is an exceptionally worthy orchid to grow in a window or fluorescent-light garden. A mature plant may be nearly everblooming and the scent of the curiously "upside-down" flowers is always welcome. Provide bright light and average temperatures.

Epidendrum ibaguense *is a terrestrial orchid found on soil and rocks in tropical America.*

Epidendrum
eh-pi-DEN-drum

- Sympodial
- Light: Medium
- Temperature: Warm to cool
- Flowering: All seasons, primarily spring to summer
- Care: Beginner

The genus epidendrum is large, but its culture is not as confusing as that of dendrobiums, another large genus.

There are two main types of epidendrum species: Those with reedlike stems and those with pseudobulbs. And, because orchids are never that simple, there are also some in-between forms. Some of the pseudobulbous epidendrums have been renamed by botanists and are now properly placed in the genus encyclia, though they may still be referred to as epidendrums in books and catalogs. Both names are listed in the following descriptions.

Reed-stem epidendrums are important cut-flower orchids in Hawaii, but most grow too tall and need too much light for indoor culture. They make wonderful garden plants where frost is not likely to occur. Epidendrums naturalize readily in such situations.

SPECIES

■ EPIDENDRUM CILIARE:
Upright pseudobulbs arising from a creeping rhizome make this plant look much like a cattleya. It usually grows to about 1 foot tall. The fragrant flowers are about 5 inches across and have yellowish green petals and sepals. The lip is white and split into three lobes. The side lobes are fringed; the center lobe is narrow and straight. *Epi. ciliare* blooms in winter and is easy to grow. It is native to Mexico and the West Indies to Colombia and Brazil.

■ EPI. ILENSE: This species was found in the latter half of the twentieth century in Ecuador and has been meristemmed at the Marie Selby Botanical Gardens, Sarasota, Florida. A reed-stem type, it continues to bloom on old and new stems, the flowers—white with narrow-fringed green sepals and petals—in nonstop, nodding clusters of five to 10.

■ EPI. PSEUDEPIDENDRUM: Originally described in 1852 as *Pseudopidendrum spectabile*, this species was transferred to epidendrum in 1856. From Costa Rica and Panama, it is a tall epiphyte with tufted stems, growing to 3 feet. The medium-sized, showy flowers have green sepals and petals while the large lip is golden yellow with orange in the throat and a white-marked purple column.

HYBRIDS

■ PSEUDOBULBOUS EPIDENDRUMS: Along with encyclias, these are often crossed with their close relatives, cattleyas. These hybrids, called epicattleyas, are usually between 4 and 8 inches tall and have 8- to 12-inch spikes of fragrant flowers. Their compact size and vivid colors make them noteworthy for light gardens.

EPIDENDRUM CULTIVARS AND HYBRIDS

Epidendrum Emerald Star
Epi. Hokulea 'Tom Wilson' AM/AOS
Epi. ilense 'Lil' HCC/AOS
Epi. Nursery Rhyme
Epi. Plastic Doll 'Lil' AM/AOS
Epi. pseudepidendrum 'Harford' AM/AOS
Epi. Tammy Virgen
Epi. Traci Sellers
Epicattleya Isler's Goldregen
Epc. Rene Marques 'Happy Harry' HCC/AOS
Epc. Princess Hitachi
Epilaelia Cinnamatica
Epl. Florence Rogers
Epilaeliocattleya Merry Green

Epidendrum vitellinum *is more correctly known as* **Encyclia vitellina.** *It blooms delightfully in spring and summer.*

TIPS FOR SUCCESS

Tolerant about soil mixes—provided they drain well—medium- to fine-grade fir bark, tree fern, or a mix of charcoal, peat, perlite, or coconut fiber can be used. If in a bark mix, use 30-10-10 fertilizer. Provide sun in morning or afternoon but some shade at midday. Height of the species suits them to gardens and greenhouses rather than windows or lights.

Laelia

LAY-lee-ah

- Sympodial
- Light: Medium to high
- Temperature: Intermediate
- Flowering: Varies
- Care: Beginner to intermediate

Laelias are closely related to cattleyas; some are so similar that it is difficult to discern the difference. Botanists distinguish between them by counting the number of pollinia; laelias have eight pollinia, and cattleyas have four.

Laelias have large, showy flowers in orange, yellow, pink, purple, and white. With their ruffled, often brightly colored and patterned lips, they resemble cattleyas, but the petals and sepals of laelias are usually narrower. Plants range in size from 3 inches to 2 feet. Compact species bear flowers on short spikes, but larger species may have 6-foot inflorescences.

Most laelias and cattleyas may be grown together. Although most laelias perform well in intermediate temperatures, some species may do best in temperatures at the cool or warm end of the intermediate range.

*Laelia anceps, **introduced from Mexico in 1835, needs high light.***

4 inches across. The sepals and petals are a rich rosy purple. The lip has a white throat.

- **L. PURPURATA:** One of the largest laelias, to 20 inches tall, it has fragrant flowers in early summer, up to 8 inches across, from white to bluish purple. The lip is usually marked with purple. Hundreds of colors and hybrids of this Brazilian species are available.

SPECIES

Laeliocattleya Chitchat 'Tangerine' makes a tremendous show in late winter and spring.

- **LAELIA ANCEPS:** Each 4- to 6-inch pseudobulb bears one leathery leaf up to 8 inches long. The flowers, to 4 inches across, are held on long stems. The sepals and petals are often pale rose-purple, but white forms are quite beautiful. The outside of the three-lobed lip matches the petals, but the inside is bright crimson-purple, with yellow and red stripes in the throat. The flowers appear in winter and last about two months on the plant; they do not last well when cut, however.

L. anceps is renowned for its endurance of high and low temperatures, withstanding spells as hot as 100° F and cold snaps when the temperature may drop to 30° F. It is native to Mexico.

- **L. PUMILA:** This delightful miniature from Brazil flowers in the fall. Oval pseudobulbs 1 inch long suppport shiny, 5-inch leaves. The flowers average 3 to

HYBRIDS

Laelia species interbreed freely and many interspecific hybrids have been produced. They contribute brilliant colors, vigorous, compact growth and, often, ease of flowering. There are laeliocattleyas (laelia × cattleya), brassolaelias (brassavola × laelia), and the trigeneric brassolaeliocattleyas, of which there are hundreds known as "Blc." *L. anceps* has parented hundreds of fine hybrids. *L. purpurata* contributes its large flowers and purple-marked labellum to many intergeneric hybrids.

TIPS FOR SUCCESS

While laelias do well along with cattleyas, it is well to remember that in general they need cooler temperatures—they will do nicely with minimum temperatures of 50°–54° F. The plants thrive outdoors in summer and on a regimen of "weakly, weekly" fertilizing in spring and summer, reduced to every other week in fall and none in winter.

The jewel orchid, Ludisia discolor, *is grown primarily for its iridescent, silky foliage.*

Ludisia
loo-DEE-see-ah

- Terrestrial
- Light: Low to medium
- Temperature: Intermediate to warm
- Flowering: Fall to winter
- Care: Beginner to intermediate

Ludisias are the most popular of the "jewel orchids," a group of spreading, ground-dwelling plants. Most jewel orchids have spikes of small, white flowers in season, most often winter to spring, but it is for their beautiful foliage they are grown. The orchid with the gorgeous leaves was first described in 1818 and given the name *Goodyera discolor.* That particular specimen was mistakenly thought to have originated in Brazil. In fact, the genus is from China and Southeast Asia,

TIPS FOR SUCCESS

The jewel orchids are unique in that they are grown for the beauty of their leaves, not for their flowers. They are superb plants for fluorescent-light gardens and for growing in a terrarium that receives bright window light but never direct sun. They are also among the few plants that on average do better in less light rather than more.

notably India, Burma, south China, Indochina to Malaya, and the Malay Archipelago. The genus name ludisia was established in 1825 and later, in the same year, another botanist named it haemaria, the name by which it was known until the mistake was brought to light in 1970 through publication of the correction in the *Kew Bulletin.*

SPECIES

■ *LUDISIA DISCOLOR (HAEMARIA DISCOLOR):* The only species in the genus, this is a low, spreading plant with 2- to 3-inch velvety, maroon leaves that have contrasting metallic red or gold veins, more pronounced in the variety *dawsoniana.* The flowers are white with twisted yellow columns, measure about ¾ inch across, and are held on an upright stalk.

Ludisias need higher humidity and warmer temperatures than most other orchids—they make superb terrarium plants. An aquarium with a glass top is ideal. To provide a balance between high humidity and air circulation, leave the top partially open; a 2-inch gap is about right. Use a well-drained, humus-rich medium, such as a commercial terrestrial orchid mix or a homemade mixture of equal parts peat moss, perlite, and potting soil. The plants may be grown in pots within the terrarium or planted directly in its bottom. If you grow the plants in pots, surround them with moist peat or sphagnum moss to maintain the humidity. Ludisia grows best in temperatures between 75° and 85° F. If the plants refuse to grow, raise the temperature inside the terrarium by adding bottom heat (see "Adding Bottom Heat," page 13), which will also increase the level of humidity.

Ludisias are surprisingly easy to propagate from cuttings of the stem, which may be broken into pieces having several nodes where leaves have grown. Lay these on moist sphagnum moss (in the manner illustrated on page 40). It is also possible to root tip cuttings, which include several healthy leaves at the growing tip. Late winter or spring or when constant warmth and high humidity can be readily provided is the ideal time.

MORE JEWEL ORCHIDS

Cultivars and hybrids of *Ludisia discolor* are rarely if ever listed. There are several other jewel orchids having beautiful foliage and which will thrive in similar growing conditions. They include:
Anoetochilus roxburghii and *A. sikkimensis* (creepers; bronze-green leaves netted gold)
Goodyera pubescens (rattlesnake plantain; pointed leaves variegated white and green; needs coolness, 50–70° F)
Macodes petola and var. *javanica,* also M. *sanderiana* (gold or silver veins in prominent patterns on dark green)

Ludisia discolor's spikes of small white flowers have a twisted, yellow column.

Masdevallia

maz-de-VAL-lee-ah

- Sympodial
- Light: Low to medium
- Temperature: Most prefer cool, some intermediate
- Flowering: Varies, most spring to summer
- Care: Beginner to advanced

The showiest parts of a masdevallia flower are the sepals. In this genus, the petals are tiny structures nestled in the center of the flower. The sepals join at the base to form a tube, which narrows toward its tip, often into long tails, making the flowers of some species resemble kites. Most forms have distinctly triangular or tubular flowers. Flower colors include pure white, green, and brownish black, but the most popular species are orange to red. Flower sizes range from about one to 10 inches. Some are pendent, others are erect.

A collection of Masdevallia ignea *orchid plants makes a cheerful, unforgettable show.*

SPECIES

If you live in an area with cool summers and can provide plenty of humidity, you can grow any of the masdevallias. *Masdevallia veitchiana*, a beauty with bright orange flowers covered with tiny fluorescent purple hairs, grows wild in the ruins of Machu Picchu in the Peruvian Andes. *Masd. coccinea*, another plant from the Andes, has a number of color forms, including scarlet, magenta, yellow, and white.

In areas with intermediate temperatures, the following species may be more successful.

■ ***MASDEVALLIA FLORIBUNDA:*** This small, tufted plant grows to about 4 inches tall. Named for its abundant flowers, it blooms from early summer to early fall. The pale yellow blossoms are about 1 inch across and are spotted with brown or purple. The tips of the sepals have a reddish tinge. It is native to Mexico, Guatemala, Honduras, and Belize; discovered by Henri Galeotii, a French botanist, near Veracruz, Mexico, in 1840.

■ ***MASDEVALLIA INFRACTA:*** This plant's tufts of leaves reach up to 8 inches. The sepals are joined at their bases to form a bell, then narrow abruptly into three outwardly

Masdevallia coccinea, *from Colombia and Peru, was discovered on the southern slopes of the Andes near Pamplona in 1842 by Jean Linden.*

Masdevallia floribunda *was the first Mexican species from this genus known to cultivation, discovered near Veracruz in 1840.*

The triangular shape and rich, velvety coloring of the scarlet masdevallias make them among the favorites of collectors.

curving tails. The flower colors vary but most are pale yellow with deep red to purple markings. *Masd. infracta* blooms from spring to summer. It is found in Brazil and Peru. Discovered by the French botanist M.E. Descourtilz near Rio de Janeiro in the 1830s, it is still a popular species today.

■ **MASDEVALLIA PERISTERIA:** This is an unusual species with leaves that are about 5 inches tall. The 4- to 5-inch flowers open wide and are green with purple spots. Their tails are relatively short (about 1½ inches long) and have a yellow tinge. The plant flowers from April to June, is native to Colombia, where it was discovered in 1873 by Gustav Wallis, who sent the plants to Messrs. Veitch & Sons in England.

■ **MASDEVALLIA TOVARENSIS:** One of the most popular masdevallias, *Masd. tovarensis* is noted for its showy flowers that look like kites. The plant grows in clumps reaching from 4 to 7 inches tall. Each long stem bears several translucent white flowers with greenish tails. The lower sepals are wide and joined for most of their length; and the upper sepal consists of little other than a narrow, upright spur. Native to Venezuela and discovered near Tovar by Jean Linden in 1842, this species blooms in winter and collectors consider it essential.

TIPS FOR SUCCESS

Masdevallias are true cloud-forest orchids, requiring constant moisture. They have no pseudobulbs—the fleshy leaves are borne on tiny stems sprouting from small rhizomes—and thus cannot endure periods without water. Most are from high elevations (between 6,000 and 12,000 feet) and need cool conditions, but a few species will grow in intermediate temperatures.

Although masdevallias need lots of humidity, excess water on the plant causes a fungal infection that rots the leaves where they join the stem. Don't try to compensate for low humidity with frequent misting or watering. If your plants do succumb to the fungus, treat them with a fungicide containing benomyl and make sure they have adequate ventilation.

Because of the need for constant high humidity, masdevallias usually cannot be grown in the house except in a fluorescent-light garden contained within a space where a humidifier can be operated at all times and where the air can be kept gently moving with an oscillating fan.

HYBRIDS

Masdevallias were all the rage in England in the late 1800s, and many growers crossed the species sent to them by New World plant explorers. Around the turn of the century, interest in masdevallia waned and few new hybrids were bred for more than 50 years.

In the last few decades, however, several orchid firms in the United States have produced some exquisite new hybrids. These breeders are combining the large flower size and bright colors of the cool-growing species with the vigorous growth and abundant blooming of the intermediate species to create stunning hybrids that are much easier to grow than their parents. Even in areas with rather hot, muggy summers, the small masdevallia plants can be accommodated by growing them under lights in an air-conditioned home or in a home greenhouse that is adequately shaded and cooled by means of an aspen-pad ("swamp") cooler, which pulls air across moistened pads.

One of the first of these new hybrids was *Masd.* Marguerite, a cross of *Masd. veitchiana* and *Masd. infracta*. According to the growers, *Masd. infracta* gives the plants vigor and the ability to tolerate intermediate temperatures, but the flowers look like those of *Masd. veitchiana*— orange with a purplish red band of tiny hairs down the centers of the sepals. *Masd. veitchiana* was first collected—by Pearce for Messrs. Veitch & Sons of England—in 1867 near Cuzco, where it was found growing in the ruins of Machu Picchu.

Masd. Angel Frost, a hybrid of *Masd. strobelii* and *Masd. veitchiana*, has two lovely forms. Both have large, open, yellow-orange flowers, but some have the tiny white hairs of *Masd. strobelii* and others have the purple hairs of *Masd. veitchiana*. A purple-haired selection, *Masd.* Angel Frost 'Mary' was awarded an HCC/AOS; its color and markings are outstanding, a masdevallia collector's dream and prime acquisition.

MASDEVALLIA CULTIVARS AND HYBRIDS

Masdevallia Bella Donna 'Willow Pond' AM/AOS
Masd. Chokkan
Masd. coccinea 'Dwarf Pink'
Masd. Copper Angel 'J&L' AM/AOS
Masd. Fuchsia Dawn
Masd. Goldie
Masd. Keiko Komoda 'Katherine' HCC/AOS
Masd. Kentucky Star
Masd. Margaret Brown
Masd. Myck Santos
Masd. Pink Pearl
Masd. Pixie Gem
Masd. schroederiana 'Don Richardson' AM-CCM/AOS
Masd. Senga
Masd. Snowkist
Masd. Ted Khoe
Masd. Watercolor Dreamer

Masdevallia veitchiana *is by nature cool-loving and suited to cultivation only in cool places.*

Miltonia
mil-TOH-nee-ah

- Sympodial
- Light: Low to medium
- Temperature: Colombian, cool; Brazilian, intermediate
- Flowering: Most summer to fall
- Care: Intermediate to advanced

Miltonias are the well-known "pansy orchids," plants with large flat flowers that look very much like their nickname. Some miltonia flowers are lightly fragrant. A part of the tribe *Oncidieae*, the approximately 20 species of miltonias are distinguished from their relatives in the odontoglossum, oncidium, and brassia genera by differences in their flowers—minor differences in some cases.

Despite the presence of their water-storing pseudobulbs, miltonias can't withstand periods of dryness. Water them as you would cymbidiums, keeping the medium moist—but not soggy—at all times. A potting mix of fine fir bark, amended with sphagnum moss, perlite, and a little charcoal provides a good balance for these moisture-loving plants. If the new leaves emerge pleated, the plant is not getting enough water. Increased watering won't flatten them out, but the next leaves should be smooth. The flowers of the Colombian species last from two weeks to two months on the plant, but wither quickly when cut. Brazilian miltonias make fine cut flowers.

This aged specimen of Miltonia spectabilis shows what is possible with devoted care.

are chestnut brown with yellow markings. The lip is shaped like an inverted spade, and is white at the bottom and violet to purple with yellow markings at the top. The plants grow between 1 and 1½ feet tall and bloom from summer to fall on 2-foot spikes. Each spike holds seven to 10 flowers.

- **MILTONIA REGNELLII:** The white sepals and petals of this species are sometimes tinted with rose. The broad, slightly undulating lip is light pink streaked with deeper pink. At the center of the lip is a prominent yellow

BRAZILIAN SPECIES

- **MILTONIA CLOWESII:** The sepals and petals of these 2- to 3-inch fragrant flowers

With its delicate coloring, Miltonia Honolulu appears to carry the genes of the family classic beauty and species type, Milt. spectabilis.

This hybrid miltonia resembles Milt. Hamburg 'Red Sky,' a red-white, spring-blooming cultivar having extra large, pansy-type flowers.

The flowers of this hybrid pansy orchid are unusually fine in their rounded, full form, and in the definition of the different colors.

structure called the callus. The flowers are generally between 2 and 3 inches across. Three to five flowers are borne on each 2-foot spike. The plant reaches 1 to 1½ feet tall. It flowers from summer to fall.

■ **MILTONIA SPECTABILIS:** The growth habit of this miltonia is a bit unruly. The pseudobulbs are spaced about an inch apart and are quickly forced over the edges of the pot by the rapid growth of the rhizome. But the flowers are splendid. Borne one to a stem, they have white sepals and petals, sometimes with a rosy tinge toward the base. The white lip is large and spreading, and has reddish purple lines radiating from the yellow callus at the center. In the variety *moreliana*, the sepals and petals match the deep reddish purple markings in the lip. The plants put on a wonderful show in late summer.

COLOMBIAN SPECIES

■ **MILTONIA VEXILLARIA (MILTONIOPSIS VEXILLARIA):** This is the most popular of the Colombian species, and appears in the pedigree of many hybrids. The plants have erect, sturdy growth to about 1 foot tall. The flowers are large—sometimes more than 4 inches across—and dazzling. The bright rose and white sepals and petals are

small in relation to the richly colored lip, which spreads out magnificently and splits into two fat lobes. The lip is mostly white, variously streaked with red and yellow. *Milt. vexillaria* flowers in the spring and summer.

BRAZILIAN HYBRIDS

In addition to increasing the number and size of the flowers, breeders of Brazilian miltonias are creating hybrids that will tolerate a wide range of temperatures. Many new hybrids contain genes of the following hybrid parents.

■ **MILTONIA ANNE WARNE:** This is the first registered Brazilian miltonia hybrid, the result of a cross made in 1949 of *Milt.* Bluntii and *Milt. spectabilis* var. *moreliana*. Its flowers are a deep purple and are held singly above the foliage. Brazilian miltonias easily form natural hybrids; *Milt.* Bluntii is one of the most important. A cross of *Milt. clowesii* and *Milt. spectabilis*, the foliage of *Milt.* Bluntii closely resembles that of *Milt. spectabilis*. The fragrant, light yellow flowers are about 3 inches long with reddish brown blotches. The lip is similar to that of *Milt. spectabilis*, but it does not come to a point. It blooms summer to fall.

COLOMBIAN HYBRIDS

These flowers have beautiful rounded shapes and bright combinations of red, pink, white, and yellow. The markings at the base of the lip, called the "mask" by breeders, are intricate and striking. In some of these hybrids, such as *Milt.* Celle, the mask is a splash of colors; hybridizers call these "waterfall masks." In the future, miltonia breeders hope to combine the traits of these cool-growing beauties with the best of the Brazilians.

INTERGENERIC HYBRIDS

Miltonias have been crossed with brassias, odontoglossums, oncidiums, and cochliodas. These hybrids are described under the genus *Odontoglossum*.

TIPS FOR SUCCESS

There are two types of miltonias, differing in flower form and cultural needs. The ones with the flat, pansy-type flowers grow in high, cool areas of Colombia and nearby countries. (These are now technically grouped in the genus miltoniopsis.) These plants do best in light intensities in the 1,000 to 1,500 footcandle range, about the same as phalaenopsis. They need cool night temperatures, however, and are sensitive to daytime highs over 80° F.

The flowers of the other type, the Brazilian miltonias, look more like odontoglossums. They prefer medium light intensities (1,500 to 3,000 footcandles) and slightly warmer temperatures.

Miltonias of both types sunburn easily. If the plants are getting enough light, the leaves will be light green, lighter than you may think is healthy if you compare them to other plants. A slight tinge of pink indicates that the plants are receiving as much light as they will tolerate. To avoid sunburn, shade the plants or move them away from windows during especially hot spells.

Miltonia spectabilis is one of the orchid world's classic beauties. It was first collected in Brazil and flowered in Birmingham, England, in 1837.

Odontoglossum
oh-don-toh-GLOSS-um

- Sympodial
- Light: Medium
- Temperature: Cool
- Flowering: Varies with species
- Care: Intermediate to advanced

The genus odontoglossum is a large one, containing approximately 300 species. Botanists have tidied up the genus by moving some of the species to the genus rossioglossum, but these orchids are still commonly called odontoglossums.

Their exquisite inflorescences are produced from the bases of the flattened pseudobulbs, and are usually erect and arching. The flowers are often large and showy, and come in shades of white, yellow, or green, marked with purple or brown blotches. They last a long time on the plant or as cut flowers.

Their showy blossoms have made odontoglossums very popular with hobbyists, despite the plants' sometimes exacting temperature requirements. Most species live high in the Andes Mountains, where they are continually bathed in cool, moist fog. They thrive in nighttime low temperatures of 45° F and daytime highs of 60° F—conditions similar to those required by cymbidiums. Outside of the Pacific Northwest, most areas of the United States are decidedly too warm for these plants. Some of the best-known species in this group are *Odontoglossum crispum*, *Odm. luteo-purpureum*, and *Odm. odoratum*. More than 1,000 distinctly different varieties of *Odm. crispum* have been named.

Odontoglossum plants typically have sculptural pseudobulbs and attractive foliage.

SPECIES

■ **ODONTOGLOSSUM PULCHELLUM:** Given time, this plant will form a large, handsome clump about 15 inches tall. The white flowers are rounded and fragrant. At the center of each flower is a yellow callus with reddish brown spots. Three to 10 flowers are borne on a slim, erect stalk in the spring. *Odm. pulchellum* is native to Mexico, Guatemala, El Salvador, and Costa Rica.

■ **ROSSIOGLOSSUM GRANDE (ODONTOGLOSSUM GRANDE):** Popularly called the "tiger orchid," its waxy flowers are anywhere in size from 5 to 9 inches across. This plant gets its common name from its

Odontioda *Durham Pride* is a stunning example of why these hybrids between odontoglossum and cochlioda are so coveted.

Lemboglossum maculatum (*aka* Odontoglossum maculatum) *is a* Mexican species from misty cloud forests, first collected in 1825.

Odontioda *Moonglow* is large and ruffled. The flowers array themselves along an arching scape and make a breathtaking show.

coloring: golden yellow with reddish brown bands and flecks. The callus is interesting; it looks like a fat little doll. The plant grows to about 15 inches tall and blooms anytime from fall to spring. It is found in Mexico and Guatemala.

HYBRIDS

Hybrids of odontoglossum with related genera such as oncidium and miltonia are much more adaptable to intermediate temperatures than are the odontoglossum species and their hybrids. In addition to growing well in a wide range of temperatures, the intergeneric hybrids have large flowers with interesting shapes and unusual colors. Although they are much more adaptable than the species from which they were bred, these intergeneric hybrids do have temperature preferences. The hybrids in the following man-made genera adapt to intermediate conditions. Some of these hybrids don't contain odontoglossum genes but are listed here for easy comparison:
- Adaglossum (ada × odontoglossum)
- Aliceara (brassia × oncidium × miltonia)
- Brassidium (brassia × oncidium)
- Colmanara (miltonia × odontoglossum × oncidium)
- Miltassia (miltonia × brassia)

TIPS FOR SUCCESS

Odontoglossums should not be allowed to dry out completely between waterings. Many growers use a mixture containing 1 part coarse sand, 1 part shredded peat, 1 part coarse perlite, and 4 parts fine bark to satisfy the plants' requirements for a moist, well-drained medium.

Repot only when necessary to replace the growing medium. Odontoglossums do not grow well if their roots are frequently disturbed. When repotting, remove the old, leafless pseudobulbs with flame-sterilized clippers. Check the cut surface of the pseudobulb for rot. Rotted areas are light to dark brown; healthy tissue is white. Remove all rotten growth and sear the cut surfaces of the healthy growths with the heated blade of the clippers before repotting.

A few odontoglossums native to lower elevations—*Odm. pulchellum, Rossioglossum grande,* aka *Odm. grande*— will tolerate cool (not cold) temperatures. These plants need cool to intermediate night temperatures but don't do well if the days are warmer than 70° F for long periods.

- Miltonidium (miltonia × oncidium)
- Odontocidium (odontoglossum × oncidium)
- Sanderara (brassia × cochlioda × odontoglossum)
- Symphodontoglossum (symphyglossum × odontoglossum)
- Wilsonara (odontoglossum × cochlioda × oncidium)
- Wingfieldara (aspasia × brassia × odontoglossum).

Of these, the aliceara, brassidiums, miltonidiums, and miltassias do fairly well in warm temperatures. Many can be grown successfully in south Florida or in other areas where high summer temperatures overwhelm odontoglossums and the cool-growing hybrids. Beauty has not been compromised in the creation of warmth-tolerant hybrids; many have received awards. One of the finest aliceara, producing 6-inch cream and brown flowers with large ruffled lips, is *Aliceara* Hawaiian Delight 'Sunshine' HCC/AOS. Brassidiums, such as *Brassidium* Florida Gem 'Sylvia' HCC/AOS, have the starry shapes of brassias and the yellow and brown markings of oncidiums.

The following hybrids often have cool-growing species in their backgrounds and thus grow better in cool conditions:
- Vuylstekeara (miltonia × cochlioda × odontoglossum)
- Odontioda (odontoglossum × cochlioda)
- Odontobrassia (odontoglossum × brassia)
- Odontonia (odontoglossum × miltonia).

Some of the finest hybrids were produced before World War II and today are available as mericlones. The spring-blooming *Vuylstekeara* Cambria 'Plush' FCC/AOS-RHS has a superb burgundy flower with a large, ruffled lip marked with intricate white patterns. Another vuylstekeara awarded an FCC/AOS is *Vuylstekeara* Edna 'Stamperland'.

Many excellent prewar odontonia hybrids are also readily available.

ODONTOGLOSSUM CULTIVARS AND HYBRIDS

Odontoglossum Bruce Cobbledick
Odm. Chetumal
Odm. Chrissy Lane
Odm. Glyndebourne Adina
Odm. Moonshine
Odm. Roy Hipkins
Odm. Spotted Leopard
Odm. Summit
Odm. Wine Butterfly
Odontioda Cranberry Leopard
Oda. Electric Joe
Oda. Joe's Drum 'Madison Heights' HCC/AOS
Odontocidium Cherry Fudge 'Swiss Mocha' AM/AOS
Odcdm. Paula Hausermann
Odontonia Drag Queen
Odontonia Laurence McLaughlin

This hybrid involving odontoglossum has the ruffling and transparent pastel coloring of an odontioda, which also involves the genus cochlioda.

Oncidium
on-SID-ee-um

- Sympodial
- Light: Medium to high
- Temperature: Intermediate
- Flowering: Varies
- Care: Beginner

Approximately 500 species make up this genus. The robust, shimmering sprays of the larger oncidiums are dramatic and elegant, and the dainty spikes of the smaller species are delightful. Yellow and brown are the predominant flower colors, but white, purple, pink, and green hues are also found.

SPECIES

■ **ONCIDIUM AMPLIATUM:** The pseudobulbs of this species are large and rounded. The leaves are about 15 inches long and may be up to 5 inches wide. Brilliant yellow flowers in spring, about 1 inch across, are borne on arching sprays up to 4 feet long. *Onc. ampliatum* is native to Guatemala, Venezuela, and Bolivia.

■ **ONCIDIUM CARTHAGENENSE:** A mule-ear oncidium, this species has thick upright leaves 6 to 24 inches long, spotted with tiny, reddish brown dots. The spikes, to 5 feet, bear ruffled purple and white flowers about an inch across in summer. Wild plants are found in southern Florida, the West Indies, and from Mexico to Venezuela and Brazil.

■ **ONCIDIUM CHEIROPHORUM:** This is a charming plant with shiny, tightly clustered

The much-loved "dancing lady" oncidium comes in many sizes and blooms profusely.

pseudobulbs. The thin leaves are short; the plants reach a height of 4 inches. The flowers—vivid yellow, waxy, and deliciously fragrant—are borne in dense clusters on 6-inch spikes from fall through winter. The species occurs in Nicaragua, Costa Rica, Panama, and in the highlands of Colombia.

■ **ONCIDIUM CRISPUM:** The large, ruffled petals of *Onc. crispum* and huge dorsal sepal are nearly as big as the lip. The sepals, petals, and lip are coppery red to greenish brown. The lip has a yellow patch at the base and crest, which

Oncidium lanceanum is a beautiful example of a mule-ear oncidium, so-called because of the formation and appearance of the sturdy leaves.

The equitant species Oncidium pulchellum is one of the easier orchids to grow and is an ideal confidence builder for beginners.

The equitant oncidium hybrids such as this one, Caesar 'Roman Flame' (Onc. Robsan × Onc. Spanish Beauty) make wonderful houseplants.

is decorated with warty red protuberances. Oval leaves are borne two to three to a pseudobulb, and reach about 9 inches long. It flowers from fall to winter and is native to Brazil.

■ **ONCIDIUM LURIDUM:** A large mule-ear type, *Onc. luridum* has stout 2-foot leaves. The branching flower stalk, about 4 feet tall, bears showy white-marked-with-rose flowers in spring. The lip is tinged with orange and the crest is yellow with a pattern of orange lines. It is native to south Florida and the West Indies, and from Mexico to Peru.

■ **ONCIDIUM MACRANTHUM:** This is one of the cyrtochilum (small-lipped) oncidiums. The flowers, in early summer, are probably the largest in the genus, spreading to 4 inches. They are held on a branched, vining stalk 8 to 12 feet long, which, if trained on a wire hoop as it develops, will form a wreath of blossoms. The flower's sepals are brown, the petals gold. The complex lip has violet side lobes and a yellow midlobe. It's found in Ecuador and in the highlands of Peru.

■ **PSYCHOPSIS PAPILIO (ONCIDIUM PAPILIO):** Often a center of attention at orchid shows, the flower looks like a large hovering insect. The dorsal sepal and petals are long and narrow, curving up and forward like antennae. The lateral sepals and lip are yellow with brown markings. The 10- to

15-inch flower spikes produce new flowers at the tip. Throughout the year as the oldest flower fades, a new one opens to take its place. Native to Peru, Venezuela, Trinidad, Colombia, and Ecuador.

■ **ONCIDIUM SPHACELATUM:** This robust species has 6-inch pseudobulbs, and its leaves grow to more than 2 feet long. The golden yellow and brown flowers—November to June—are held on an upright, branched inflorescence. The side branches are longest at the bottom and shortest at the top, giving the stalk of flowers an appealing symmetry similar to that of an espalier. Native to tropical America, Mexico, Honduras, Guatemala, and El Salvador.

■ **ONCIDIUM SPLEDIDUM:** One of the largest mule-ear oncidiums, the leaves are about 3 feet tall. The showy flowers, in spring to early summer, are 3 inches across, with lemon yellow and brown sepals and petals. The large, clear yellow lip is smooth and rounded. Found in Guatemala and Honduras.

■ **ONCIDIUM TIGRINUM:** The greenish yellow and brown sepals of these fragrant, 2-inch flowers on 2-foot spikes in autumn provide a dark background for the striking yellow lip. The narrowed portion in the center of the lip lends it an asymmetrical, dumbbell shape. It is found in Mexico.

■ **ONCIDIUM TRIQUETRUM:** The thick, three-sided leaves overlap at the base and are arranged in a fan about 3 inches tall. The petals and lip of the 1-inch flowers are white, dotted with maroon. The contrasting sepals are greenish brown, lighter around the edges. Five to 15 flowers are borne on each 7-inch spike. This species usually blooms in summer, but some specimens are practically everblooming. Don't cut the spikes after flowering; they often branch and bloom again. It is native to Jamaica.

■ **ONCIDIUM VARICOSUM:** The name "dancing dolls" is applied to numerous other oncidiums, but it describes this pseudobulbous species best of all. The fall-winter, yellow-and-brown flowers dance like ballerinas in troupes of 200 on lacily branched stems up to 5 feet long.

TIPS FOR SUCCESS

Unlike their relatives in the genera odontoglossum and miltonia, oncidium species are generally easy to grow, adapting well to intermediate temperatures and tolerating an occasional missed watering without damage.

Oncidium crispum and Onc. macranthum grow best in temperatures at the cool end of the intermediate range.

The equitant oncidiums have a long-standing reputation as outstanding houseplants and confidence builders. In fact, most interspecific oncidium hybrids are equitants. One of the first equitant hybrids was *Onc. Golden Glow*, a cross of *Onc. triquetrum* and *Onc. urophyllum*. *Onc. Golden Sunset*, another fairly old hybrid, is the result of the combination of four species: *Onc. pulchellum*, *Onc. triquetrum*, *Onc. urophyllum*, and *Onc. guianense*.

The equitants as well as oncidiums in general get along well outdoors in summer, benefitting from rain or, in its absence, showering with the hose. Bring them inside before temperatures drop below 50° F.

Oncidium ampliatum var. majus *is a much-loved winter-flowering, yellow species. It needs intermediate to warm temperatures and is easy to grow indoors.*

Paphiopedilum

paff-ee-oh-PED-i-lum

- Sympodial
- Light: Low to medium, depending on species
- Temperature: Intermediate to cool, depending on species
- Flowering: Generally fall to spring
- Care: Beginner to advanced

Paphiopedilums differ from other orchids in the appearance of the plants as well as their flowers. One of the most obvious features that sets the flowers apart is the lip, which is modified into a pouch, like a cup. This pouch suggests the name "lady's slipper," a common name applied to paphiopedilums and their relatives in the subfamily *Cypripedioideae*.

Another exceptionally showy part of a paphiopedilum flower is the dorsal (uppermost) sepal, which is usually shaped like an upside-down heart and colorfully marked with distinct lines or spots.

The two lower sepals are fused into one, and may be almost completely hidden behind the pouch. The long, narrow petals stick straight out at the sides of the flower or may hang down like a long mustache. Tufts of black hairs sprout from the upper edges of the petals in some species.

All of the flower parts are thick and waxy, taking on the texture of rubbery plastic in the modern hybrids. Green, brown, white, and pink hues predominate in the species; the hybrids may also contain vivid shades of red and purple. These colors may be subtly

Paphiopedilum chamberlainianum (left) and Paph. *Papa Rohl* dressed for display in baskets.

blended or patterned in bold stripes and spots.

Paphiopedilum flowers are usually borne singly atop thick stalks, but a few species bear as many as six flowers on a single stalk.

Paphiopedilums also have a unique growth habit. Unlike most orchids, which live in the bright sunlight of the treetops, paphiopedilums are terrestrials, living in the shade of the forest floor. Because this environment is always moist, these plants have no water-storing stems or pseudobulbs. Their leathery leaves join at the base of the plant, forming fans of three to seven leaves. The leaves may be pure green or mottled with silvery or light and dark green. Green-leaved paphiopedilums

This imposing and surreal, waxy flower is typical of those produced by the green-leaved and cooler growing hybrid paphiopedilums.

Paphiopedilum callosum *flowers in spring and summer above the beautifully variegated leaves, bluish, silvery green with darker mottling.*

Paphiopedilum *St. Swithin* is one of the remarkably beautiful green-and-white lady's slipper orchids. It's a superb plant for the beginner.

and mottled-leaved paphiopedilums have different temperature requirements. Species and hybrids with green leaves generally need cool night temperatures, especially in the fall when the flower buds are in the process of developing. Plants with mottled leaves bloom freely in intermediate night temperatures. Day temperatures between 70° and 80° F are ideal for both types.

Both types of paphiopedilum also do well in light intensities ranging from 800 to 1,200 footcandles (see page 7). The light intensity should be at the low end of the range in the summer when temperatures are high so that the plants don't dry out too quickly. Leaf yellowing may be a sign of too much light. The foliage of the green-leaved forms should be a medium green; the darker patches in mottled-leaf forms should be dark green.

Paphiopedilums are excellent orchids for fluorescent-light gardens. Their undemanding light and temperature requirements and free-blooming habits also make the mottled-leaved paphiopedilums some of the best orchids for the beginning window gardener. Not only do the plants bloom frequently and with no special treatment, the flowers last in perfect form on the plant or in a vase for at least a month; some last up to three months. Their attractive foliage makes them decorative even

when they are not in bloom.

Paphiopedilums are best when allowed to grow into large specimen plants. They may be divided if they grow too large, die out in the center, or if you simply want more plants. It is better to break (rather than cut) the plants apart, creating divisions with at least three growths.

Paphiopedilums don't respond well to meristem culture. Most of the plants on the market are seedlings or very old cultivars that have been multiplied through conventional division.

MOTTLED-LEAVED SPECIES

■ *PAPHIOPEDILUM BELLATULUM:* The dark green leaves of this unusual species are sparingly mottled on their upper surfaces and have purple spots below. The inflorescence is so short that the flowers are borne right on top of the leaves. The entire flower is white or pale yellow and is liberally spotted with purplish brown. Unlike those of most other paphiopedilums, the petals of this species are rounded and are larger than the dorsal sepal. It blooms in spring, and is native to Burma and Thailand. This is an exceptionally fine orchid for growing in a fluorescent-light garden because it remains short, even when in flower. Messrs. Low & Co. of Clapton, England, first introduced *Paph. bellatulum* into cultivation in 1888.

■ *PAPHIOPEDILUM CALLOSUM:* The leaves of this species are a light bluish-green with darker mottling. The long-lived flowers are about 4 inches across. They have a large, rounded dorsal sepal that is white and green with purple streaks. The petals point downward at a 45-degree angle. They are greenish at the base and suffused with purple at the tips. The lip is brownish purple.

This species flowers in spring to summer. It is native to Thailand, Laos, and Cambodia. It was

PAPHIOPEDILUM CULTIVARS AND HYBRIDS

Paphiopedilum ang thong var. *album* 'Dragon' AM/AOS

Paph. Fanaticum 'Wedgwood' AM/AOS

Paph. glanduliferum 'Truford' HCC/AOS

Paph. Harold Koopowitz 'Robert Weltz' FCC/AOS

Paph. insigne var. *sanderae* 'Hall's Classic' FCC/AOS

Paph. Magic Lantern 'Pink Passion' HCC/AOS

Paph. malipoense 'Blumen Insel IV' HCC/AOS

Paph. micranthum 'A&P II' AM/AOS

Paph. rothschildianum 'Renate Stern' AM/AOS

TIPS FOR SUCCESS

Although paphiopedilums grow on the ground and are classified as terrestrials, their roots usually do not penetrate the soil, but ramble instead through the moist, well-aerated humus on the surface. You can simulate this root environment with a variety of potting mediums; fine fir bark amended with a little perlite is a tried-and-true mixture. Plants should be watered frequently enough to keep them moist but not soggy. Plastic pots are generally used to help retain moisture.

When watering paphiopedilums, avoid splashing water into the growing points and leaf axils. If water collects and remains in these places for long, a bacterial rot can kill the growing points and young leaves. Overzealous misting can also cause bacterial infections. Paphiopedilums are sensitive to salt accumulations. Leach the medium occasionally with plain water and don't overdo with fertilizer.

Species and hybrids with green leaves need cool night temperatures, especially in the fall when the flower buds are set.

Paphiopedilum insigne *is a green-leaved lady's slipper that needs cool night temperatures. The flowers, up to 5 inches, are sometimes carried two to a stem—most impressive!*

Paphiopedilum sukhakulii *is outstanding for a houseplant collection.*

PAPHIOPEDILUM
continued

discovered by Alexandre Regnier of Paris in Thailand in Indochina and introduced into cultivation in 1885.

■ *PAPHIOPEDILUM SUKHAKULII:* This species' leaves are dark green and mottled with light green. The dorsal sepal is pale green with well-defined lines of much darker green. The petals are stiff, nearly flat, and point slightly downward. They are pale green, spotted all over with dark purple. The lip of this exotic and unusual species is pale green, mottled, and veined with purple. The flowers are produced in summer. It occurs in Thailand and was introduced first in Germany in 1964.

■ *PAPHIOPEDILUM VENUSTUM:* The leaves of this species are particularly attractive. The upper surfaces are dark green with pale mottling; the undersides are dark purplish green. The dorsal sepal is white with green lines. The petals are similarly colored at their bases, but the ends look as if they have been dipped in red lacquer and their wavy edges bristle with black hairs. The lip is orange to bronze and is veined with green. It blossoms from late winter to early summer and grows wild in Nepal, Bangladesh, and India. It was one of the first paphiopedilum species introduced into the West, in England in 1819. Subsequently, *Paph. venustum* was one of the first orchid species to be hybridized when, in 1871, a Mr. Cross, gardener to Lady Ashburton of Melchett Court, Hampshire, England, crossed it with *Paph. insigne* to create *Paph.* Crossii.

GREEN-LEAVED SPECIES

■ *PAPHIOPEDILUM FAIRIEANUM:* This small plant has ornate flowers about 2 inches across. The dorsal sepal is white with violet lines and netting. It is notably large in proportion to the rest of the flower and has wavy edges. The upward-curling petals have the same pattern and coloration as the lip but with the addition of a greenish tinge. The green and violet lip has purple veins. It blooms from summer to early fall. *Paph. fairieanum* occurs in India (Assam, Sikkim) and was introduced into cultivation by a Mr. Fairrie of Liverpool, England, in 1857.

■ *PAPHIOPEDILUM INSIGNE:* Although this species sometimes bears two flowers on a stem, most of the time it produces a single 4- to 5-inch blossom. The brownish tinge and shiny surface of its apple-green flowers make them look as if they've been varnished. The dorsal sepal is yellow to light green with slightly darker green lines and brown to purple spots. The undulating petals and helmet-shaped lip have a color scheme similar to that of the dorsal sepal, but with more brown or purple. It may flower at any time from fall to spring.

Like most of the other green-leafed paphiopedilums, this species is native to India and Nepal. It first flowered in the West in 1820 in the Liverpool Botanic Garden. An albino form, var. *sanderae*, is entirely yellowish green, the dorsal sepal having a white margin and the flower lacking the brown pigmentation of the species.

■ *PAPHIOPEDILUM PHILIPPINENSE:* The dorsal sepals of these pleasingly triangular flowers are white with reddish-brown lines. The long, twisted reddish-purple petals are the most striking aspects of the flower, dangling to 6 inches below the center of the flower. The lip is yellow with faint brown markings, a stunning contrast to the rest of the blossom. It blooms from summer to autumn, and is native to the Philippines. It was discovered by English plantsman J.G. Veitch on Guimaras Island in 1865. This species typically occurs in the wild near the sea on limestone and even on the roots of other plants, such as *Vanda batemanii*.

HYBRIDS

■ *PAPHIOPEDILUM MAUDIAE:* Without a doubt the best paphiopedilum—some say the best orchid—for the beginner. Its beautiful mottled foliage, superb flowers, and ability to thrive in low light and average home temperatures make this hybrid one of the beginning orchid grower's best bets.

Paph. Maudiae was first produced in 1900 by a cross of the *album* (white and green) forms of *Paph. lawrenceanum* and *Paph. callosum*. These *album* forms of *Paph.* Maudiae, still popular and widely available, have white dorsal sepals with clearly defined, bright green veins. The white-tipped petals are light green with veins of darker green. The pouch is yellow-green with faint green venation. The flowers are borne on long stems above the light and dark green mottled foliage, and last for two to three months.

Paph. Maudiae 'Dorothy Ann' is a typical *album* hybrid. Two of the most popular named selections of *Paph.* Maudiae available today are 'Magnificum' and 'The Queen'. The huge, well-shaped flowers of 'The Queen' earned it an Award of Merit from the American Orchid

Graceful bearing and large bloom is typical of mottled-leaved hybrids.

Society and a First Class Certificate from the Royal Horticultural Society. Don't pass up a chance to grow one of these plants.

Not all *Paph.* Maudiae hybrids have green and white flowers. Two other color forms, *coloratum* and vinicolor, are also available.

The *coloratum* forms, produced by crossing normally pigmented *Paph. lawrenceanum* and *Paph. callosum* plants, have red flowers with darker red veins. Tufts of jet black hairs sprout from the upper edges of the petals. 'Los Osos' and 'St. Francis' are excellent cultivars of the *coloratum* forms; all have earned Awards of Merit from the American Orchid Society.

The richly hued vinicolor forms are the latest of the Maudiae hybrids. Their flowers are a deep burgundy; some are nearly black with purple-red pigments. The heavy coloration comes from two cultivars of *Paph. callosum*, 'Jac' and 'Sparkling Burgundy'.

In order to be classed as a vinicolor and not merely as a deeply hued *coloratum*, the flower must be a clear purple-red without a trace of brown, and the tip of the pouch must be nearly black. Fortunately, excellent vinicolor cultivars have come down from their sky-high pricing, which has helped them to become extremely popular. 'Diamond Jubilee' is an excellent vinicolor, earning a First Class Certificate.

Paph. Maudiae has been crossed with species paphiopedilums to produce stunning results. For example, *Paph.* Faire-Maude, a cross of *Paph.* Maudiae and *Paph. fairieanum*, is best described as a Maudiae with an oriental look.

Paph. Makuli (*Paph. sukhakulii* × *Paph.* Maudiae) has the straight, simple lines of *Paph. sukhakulii* and the easygoing cultural requirements of *Paph.* Maudiae.

There are many hybrids in the green-leaved group, such as *Paph.* Sioux 'Teal'. Often grown for cut flowers, they tend to have exceptionally large, rounded flowers with a heavy, rubbery texture.

CULTURAL NEEDS

In its most commendable, ongoing efforts to provide the general public with practical, reliable how-to information about orchids, the American Orchid Society has issued a basic cultural bulletin about paphiopedilums. These are the most important points to bear in mind:

■ **LIGHT:** Sufficient light is important for healthy growth and flower production. Provide bright light, no direct sun. In the home, an east, west, or shaded south window is best. In a greenhouse, plants need about 30 percent full sun. Under lights, use four 40-watt fluorescent tubes and two 40-watt incandescent bulbs directly over the plants. Foliage should be naturally semierect and firm, not drooping. Dark green, limp foliage indicates too little light.

■ **TEMPERATURE:** Mature plants need a 15° to 20° F temperature difference between night and day. Provide nights of 55° to 60° F and days of 70° to 85° F. Seedlings require temperatures to be 5° to 10° F warmer than mature plants.

■ **WATER:** Mature plants should never dry out between waterings. Seedlings need even more constant attention to moisture.

■ **HUMIDITY:** Paphiopedilums require humidity to range between 60 and 70 percent. In the home, place plants on trays of moistened pebbles if conditions are too dry. In a greenhouse, use a humidifier.

■ **FERTILIZER:** Paphiopedilums are more likely to grow and flower on a low-fertilizer diet than are most other orchids. However, because potting mediums provide few nutrients, you really should fertilize your plants on a regular basis. Which fertilizer to use depends on the mix in which the plant is growing. A good rule to follow is to apply a balanced fertilizer, such as 10-10-10 or 12-12-12, "weakly, weekly." Dilute the fertilizer to one-fourth the rate recommended on the product label and apply once a week.

■ **POTTING:** Repot paphiopedilums every one to two years, before the mix breaks down too far. You can repot them at almost any time of year. Use a well-drained but water-retentive mix.

Green-leaved paphiopedilums typically have compact habit and rounded, full flowers.

Phalaenopsis
fal-en-OPP-sis

- ■ Monopodial
- ■ Light: Low
- ■ Temperature: Intermediate to warm
- ■ Flowering: Fall to winter, some year-round
- ■ Care: Beginner

How could such sublimely beautiful orchids be so easy to grow? Phalaenopsis orchids, commonly called "moth orchids" for their enchanting white flowers, are some of the easiest for the beginner. Like the mottled-leaved paphiopedilums, phalaenopsis plants thrive in intermediate to warm temperatures and low light. Their low, compact growth makes them ideal windowsill plants, and they fit perfectly under fluorescent lights. Add to this easy culture their attractive foliage and beautiful long-lasting blossoms and it is easy to see why they're so popular.

Unlike most of the orchids discussed and illustrated in this book, phalaenopsis plants are monopodial, producing new leaves at the top of the plant year after year, rather than producing new growth from the base. In theory, this should make them grow taller and taller without spreading out but, because the lower leaves usually tend to die and fall off as the plant grows taller, most growers "top" their plants and repot the upper portion long before the plant reaches 1 foot tall.

Although the leafy part of a phalaenopsis plant is low and compact, the flower spikes of popular species and hybrids are erect and arching, reaching between 2 and 3 feet tall.

Botanically speaking, the largest and most popular moth orchids belong in a section of the genus *Phalaenopsis* also called Phalaenopsis. The species in this section include *Phal. amabilis*, *Phal. schilleriana*, and *Phal. stuartiana*. The flowers in section Phalaenopsis have broad, thin petals that are usually larger than the sepals, sometimes covering the space between them and giving the flowers their graceful rounded appearance. Another feature that distinguishes the plants in this section is the lip, which is tipped with a pair of appendages that resemble antennae.

The blooming season is usually from winter to

Phalaenopsis Maraldee 'Krull Smith' is a rich source for the colors known as art shades or "sunset"— pastels of unusual beauty in large flowers.

Graceful, showy, and long-lasting, it is no wonder phalaenopsis are among the most loved flowers for display in public gardens.

spring. When the flowers fade, cut the stalk just below the node that produced the first flower. If all goes well, the stem will branch and flower again. In this way, plants can be kept in bloom for months.

The plants in another section, Stauroglottis, have foliage similar to that of plants in section Phalaenopsis, but the flowers are thicker, star-shaped, and borne in short, drooping inflorescences. Although these plants are not grown as commonly as are the large hybrids, their bright colors and generous blooming habits should earn them a place in any orchid collection.

Most of these species have their peak flowering season in the summer, but they keep producing new flowers at the ends of the inflorescences for years, a wonderful phenomenon called "successive flowering." As the flowers bloom, fade, and fall off, their bracts remain on the flower stem, giving old inflorescences an interesting saw-toothed appearance. Eventually, the end of the inflorescence will stop producing flowers and turn brown. The entire inflorescence can then be removed.

Like paphiopedilums, phalaenopsis plants don't have pseudobulbs, so they are more sensitive to low humidity or a dry growing medium than are the pseudobulbous orchids such as cattleyas. Keep the bark moist but not soggy, and try to maintain a high humidity.

Also, like paphiopedilums, phalaenopsis orchids can be infected with a bacterial rot if water stands in the center of the plant or in the leaf axils for long periods of time. This rot is particularly disastrous for a phalaenopsis plant because it can kill the one and only growing point. To prevent the rot, water and mist the plants in the morning so that the excess water will evaporate quickly. If you want to be absolutely certain that the plants are safe from rot, check them at nightfall on the days that you've watered. If water is still in the growing point, gently soak it up with a twisted piece of tissue or paper towel.

Phalaenopsis plants are more difficult to propagate than are most other orchids because they can't be divided. However, many plants such as *Phal. lueddemanniana* and its hybrids produce keikis (see page 40) at the ends of their inflorescences. You can remove these and pot them up individually once they have a few well-developed roots. If keikis don't form on their own, you can induce them by removing the bracts from the nodes at the end of the flower stem and treating the buds with a hormone paste for keikis (see "Orchid Resources," page 92). Most of the time the paste makes the bud grow into a keikis, although sometimes it forms flowers or a lump of callus instead. Sometimes old plants produce keikis at their bases; these can be removed and potted like flower-stem keikis. Old, leggy plants can be topped to form two

or more new plants. This procedure is the same as for other monopodial orchid plants (see pages 37 to 39 for instructions).

SPECIES

■ ***PHALAENOPSIS AMABILIS:*** This species and several of its varieties were used to breed large white hybrid moth orchids. In fact, in the last quarter of the twentieth century, the hybrids have become so popular that it is often difficult to find specimens of the species. The flowers of *Phal. amabilis* are up to 3 inches across and have pure white sepals and petals. The intricate lip is yellow and white, striped, and spotted with red. The clawlike antennae on the lip identify it as a member of the section Phalaenopsis. *Phal. amabilis* usually blooms from October to January. It is native to Indonesia, northern Australia, New Guinea, and the Philippines.

■ ***PHALAENOPSIS AMBOINENSIS:*** One of the most striking yellow-flowered species in the *Amboinensis* section, the petals and sepals of this species are marked with bold reddish-brown patterns. The flowers are very substantial—almost leathery—and measure about 2 inches across. They are borne in succession on spikes that may reach 18 inches in length. It blooms in spring and grows wild on the island of Ambon, west of New Guinea.

■ ***PHALAENOPSIS LUEDDEMANNIANA:*** This species has confounded orchid botanists, who can't agree on whether to call it a single species with a number of different color forms or to divide it into a number of separate species. Some horticulturists, taking a conservative stance to avoid confusion in hybrid registration, continue to view *Phal. lueddemanniana* as a single species with several color forms. Herman Sweet, whose taxonomy of this genus is most widely accepted, has placed several of the forms in separate species.

Two of the most common forms placed by Herman Sweet into separate species are *Phal. hieroglyphica* and *Phal. pulchra*. The flowers of *Phal. hieroglyphica* are yellow with clusters of brown dots on the sepal and petals. *Phal. pulchra* has vivid magenta-purple flowers.

One of the most common forms Sweet has left in *Phal. lueddemanniana* is the variety *ochracea*. Its flowers are yellow with a suffusion of pale purple. If you wish to formulate your own opinion on the naming of these plants, you can find them all blooming in the spring in the Philippines.

■ ***PHALAENOPSIS SCHILLERIANA:*** The leaves of this species are particularly attractive—dark green mottled with silvery gray, usually with a tinge of magenta underneath. In ideal conditions with

Although orchid flowers such as this phalaenopsis look beautiful with droplets of rainwater on them, generally, it is best not to mist or spray water on orchid flowers.

PHALAENOPSIS
continued

sufficient humidity, they may reach over 12 inches long and 5 inches wide. Hundreds of the 2½-inch flowers may be carried on the long, drooping sprays. The color of the sepals and petals varies somewhat, but most are white with a rosy blush. The base of the large spreading lip is spotted with red and the disk at the center is golden yellow.

Phal. schilleriana is an old favorite and is very easy to grow. It usually blooms in spring and is found in the Philippines.

■ **PHALAENOPSIS STUARTIANA:** This species is similar to *Phal. schilleriana*, but its leaves are smaller and narrower. The flowers are white and, though similar in shape to those of *Phal. schilleriana*, are tinged on the lip and lower portions of the bottom sepal with golden-yellow and marked with reddish-brown patches. In some plants the upper sepal and petals have spotty patches at their bases.

This plant is recommended as exceptional for beginners because it is easy to grow and its winter-blooming flowers last a particularly long time. Like the other moth orchids, it is native to the Philippines.

■ **PHALAENOPSIS VIOLACEA:** This is more difficult to grow than most other *Phalaenopsis* species, but its flowers are lovely. They are borne on stout, 5-inch stems. This shortness has made the species popular for growing in fluorescent-light gardens. The flowers open successively over a long period; at any given time during the blooming season two or three fragrant flowers will be displayed. The top sepal and petals are mostly greenish white, but the lower half is suffused with pink to purplish rose. It flowers from spring through summer. *Phal. violacea* is native to Borneo and Malaysia.

HYBRIDS

The hybrids with large, rounded, white flowers now offered everywhere from florist's shops to grocery stores to home improvement centers—what better way to improve your home?—can all be traced back to *Phal. amabilis*. Through years of breeding, the sepals and petals have been enlarged so that they overlap to give the flower a more rounded form and have been thickened to make them sturdier and longer lasting. The overall size of the flowers has also been enlarged from the 3-inch spread found in the species to saucer-sized monsters measuring more than 5 inches, tip to tip, across the sepals.

When it became apparent that the white forms had been "perfected," phalaenopsis breeders turned to producing colorful hybrids. Many of the pink-flowered plants now commonly available get their large rounded forms from *Phal. amabilis* and their coloration from *Phal. sanderiana* and *Phal. schilleriana*. Others result from crosses of *Phal. amabilis* with *Phal. violacea*, which, in addition to making the petals and sepals pink, thickens the flower parts, shortens the inflorescence, and reduces the number of flowers.

The yellow-flowered *Phal. lueddemanniana* was crossed with white complex hybrids to produce creamy yellow flowers with pink spots such as *Phal.* Golden Sands.

Candy stripe phalaenopsis are a fairly recent development. Besides pink or rose on a white background, there also are yellow candy stripes. For example, Phalaenopsis Melinda Weber 'Magic Web.' Doritaenopsis Carrie Hillegonds 'Candy Crazy' is a dark lavender-blush candy stripe.

Breeders have also added the "tiger bars" of *Phal. amboinensis* to white-flowered hybrids to make the yellow and pink flowers of *Phal.* Solar Flare.

Most of the latest headlines in phalaenopsis breeding concern the red-flowered hybrids. *Phal. violacea* and *Phal. amboinensis* figure in the genetic backgrounds of these striking flowers, but other species with pink or yellow flowers are used as well.

Intergeneric hybrids that include phalaenopsis are also becoming quite common. One of the most important is doritaenopsis, the result of phalaenopsis being crossed with *Doritis pulcherrima*, which has rose-pink to deep purple flowers borne on an upright, well-branched stalk up to 3 feet tall. Doritaenopsis hybrids have smaller, often more deeply colored flowers than those of the phalaenopsis parent. The upright inflorescence of doritis also appears in the progeny, improving the presentation of the blooms. The hybrids grow under the same easy conditions as do phalaenopsis plants.

Visit any orchid grower who offers an up-to-date selection of phalaenopsis and you will see that an amazing array of color has been brought to the fore in this branch of the orchid family. *Doritaenopsis* Deborah Wilson 'Dear' is intense, velvety red-brown with a red lip. *Phalaenopsis* Mulberry 'Icee' is lavender with white webbing—tessellation—and a thin white edging. *Asconopsis* Irene Dobkin 'York' HCC/AOS is apricot, from crossing *Ascocentrum miniatum* × *Phalaenopsis* Doris. At first glance it looks like phalaenopsis— but the label tells the difference.

Modern phalaenopsis bloom for months on end, often branching and continuing for such a long time they are, for all practical purposes, everblooming.

PHALAENOPSIS CULTIVARS AND HYBRIDS

There are staggering numbers of new phalaenopsis cultivars and hybrids introduced every year. Besides whites as pure as the driven snow, there are whites with a colored lip, pinks, candy stripes, yellows, golds, reds, and on into "sunset" and "art" shades. A recent class, the multifloras, produce branching stems of miniature flowers that can be nearly everblooming.

TIPS FOR SUCCESS

Generally speaking, phalaenopsis are better house and greenhouse plants in temperate climates, while they can be grown outdoors in tropical regions and in the warmer parts of subtropical climates: Florida, along the Gulf Coast, southern California, and Hawaii. Phalaenopsis, the closely related doritis, and their hybrids, doritaenopsis, do well in the same conditions that produce beautiful African violets They adapt to bright window light (with little or no direct sun) or fluorescent light (at least two 40-watt tubes) and consistently warm temperatures. A slight cooling at night in the fall, to around 55° F, encourages spiking in some. Consistency with watering—no extremes of wet or dry—and fertilizing ("weekly, weakly") keeps the handsome foliage in perfect condition and helps fend off the scale insects that seem attracted to stressed phalaenopsis.

Phragmipedium

frag-mi-PEE-dee-um

- Sympodial
- Light: Medium to high
- Temperature: Intermediate
- Flowering: Spring to fall
- Care: Beginner to intermediate

Closely related paphiopedilums lack the softness and grace of phragmipediums but have similar pink flowers.

PHRAGMIPEDIM CULTIVARS AND HYBRIDS

Phragmipedium Alice
Phrag. George Shearing
Phrag. Sarah Eadie
Phrag. besseae (for brilliant red flowers) 'Memoria Mary Lou Dundon' AM/AOS
Phrag. besseae 'Neon Fire' AM/AOS
Phrag. besseae var. *flavum* 'Rising Sun' AM/AOS
Phrag. Firestorm (*Phrag. besseae* × Ruby Slippers)
Phrag. Hanne Popow 'Flamingo Dance' HCC/AOS
Phrag. Hanne Popow 'Isle of Jersey' FCC/AOS
Phrag. Memoria Dick Clements 'Red Glow' HCC/AOS

Phragmipediums are Latin American relatives of the Asian paphiopedilums (the lip forms a pouch). The dorsal petal of the phragmipedium isn't as broad and brightly marked as a paphiopedilum, but the lateral petals may be fantastically long, in some cases dangling over 2 feet. In the wild, these petals may serve as ladders for pollinating insects.

Several flowers are borne on each stalk. The leathery leaves arch gracefully upward and outward from the base. There are no pseudobulbs. Phragmipediums need brighter light than paphiopedilums, 2,400 to 3,000 footcandles. About 20 species have been discovered, varying from terrestrial plants that grow in the moist, well-drained loam of stream banks to true epiphytes that live in trees or on mossy rocks, where they enjoy high humidity.

The individual flowers are waxy, yellow and green with rose markings. They measure about 8 inches across. The flowering season is usually autumn. It is native to Panama, Costa Rica, and Colombia.

SPECIES

PHRAGMIPEDIUM CAUDATUM:
Commonly called the "mandarin orchid," this species' epiphytic habit makes it forgiving of an occasional drought. For this reason, it is recommended as the best phragmipedium for window culture. The flower stalk grows to about 2 feet tall and holds one to six flowers. The dorsal sepal is about 6 inches long and is pale yellow with light green veins. The petals are crimson, dangling up to 3 feet like narrow twisted ribbons. The slipper-shaped lip is yellowish white, and the most popular forms have crimson markings around the rim of the lip. *Phrag. caudatum* blooms at any time from spring to fall. Native Mexico to Peru.

PHRAGMIPEDIUM LONGIFOLIUM: This terrestrial has long, narrow leaves to 32 inches. The flower stalk may bear more than 10 blossoms, produced in succession over a long period.

Despite their delicate appearance, phragmipedium flowers can last up to several weeks, if not for months.

HYBRIDS

Many phragmipedium hybrids have been created. Most of the hybridizing involves *Phrag. schlimii*, a terrestrial with rounded pink and white flowers. *Phrag. caudatum* and *Phrag. longifolium* have been crossed to produce *Phrag.* Grande, a very handsome plant with green and white flowers marked with pinkish brown. As in other hybrid grexes (the offspring of a cross), in some cases the petals are long and dangling like *Phrag. caudatum*; in others, they are relatively short and stiff as in *Phrag. longifolium*.

TIPS FOR SUCCESS

Pot terrestrial species, such as *Phrag. longifolium*, in a mix of sand and peat, or in sphagnum moss. Epiphytes, such as *Phrag. caudatum*, grow well in fir bark or tree-fern fiber. The terrestrials need constant moisture and perfect drainage; the epiphytes are not harmed if the medium dries out slightly between waterings.

Sophronitis coccinea *may be a diminutive orchid but it has had a big impact in breeding.*

Sophronitis
(sof-roh-NIGH-tiss)

- Sympodial
- Light: Medium
- Temperature: Intermediate
- Flowering: Fall to winter
- Care: Intermediate to advanced

Sophronitis species are best known for the scarlet-red they contribute to the flowers of hybrid cattleyas and laeliocattleyas, but their diminutive size and well-formed blossoms make the plants worthwhile collectibles. All sophronitis are native to Brazil, where they cling to moist, mossy rocks and dead tree branches. Some species, such as *Soph. cernua*, grow at low elevations and thus tolerate temperatures at the warm end of the intermediate range. *Soph. coccinea*, the most

popular species, is from higher altitudes and suited to the low end of the intermediate range. The light requirements of sophronitis are similar to those of cattleyas. They adapt to a wide range but flower best in bright light. Sophronitis plants can be propagated by division, but they are best allowed to grow into specimen plants.

SPECIES

■ **SOPHRONITIS CERNUA:** The flat, tightly clustered pseudobulbs of this species bear rigid oval leaves about 1 inch long. Its bright red flowers are borne in clusters of two to five blossoms, each about 1 inch across. A yellow-orange patch decorates the base of the lip and column. It blooms in the winter.

■ **SOPHRONITIS COCCINEA:** The pseudobulbs and leaves of *S. coccinea* are a little longer and narrower than those of *Soph. cernua*, but the plants are still only between 2 and 4 inches tall. The flowers are borne singly and vary a great deal in size and color. Most have flowers that are about 1 to 2 inches across, but in some forms, the flowers may reach 3 inches. Colors range from a rare yellow through shades of orange to scarlet and rosy purple. The lip is usually orange with scarlet streaks. The flowers appear in fall and winter from the newest mature growths.

HYBRIDS

Sophronitis orchids are related to laelias and cattleyas. Breeders interested in creating red hybrid cattleyas began crossing sophronitis with species cattleyas and with hybrids of laeliocattleyas. Sophronitis prefer the cool end of the intermediate range. Sophrolaelias combine the compact habit and vivid colors of sophronitis with the attractive flower shapes and free-blooming habit of the laelias. These plants thrive under fluorescent lights. Sophrolaeliocattleyas (Slc.) are widely grown hybrids involving laelias, sophronitises, and cattleyas. The flowers of these small plants run the gamut from clear yellow to cherry red.

SOPHRONITIS CULTIVARS AND HYBRIDS

Sophronitis Arizona 'Spring Grand'
Sophrocattleya Calypso
Sc. Cosmo-Betty
Sophrolaelia Psyche 'China' AM/AOS
Sophrolaeliocattleya Frolic 'Apricot Magic'
Slc. Fusion
Slc. Hazel Boyd 'Apricot Glow' HCC/AOS
Slc. Jeweler's Art 'Burma Ruby' HCC/AOS
Slc. Tiny Titan JC/AOS
Potinara (Brassavola × Cattleya × Laelia × Sophronitis) Beau Moon
Pot. Memoria Shel Newberger
Pot. Pastushin's Pay Dirt

Sophronitis brevipedunculata *blooms in fall and needs cool temperatures.*

TIPS FOR SUCCESS

Sophronitis are touchy about water. They must have high humidity and a moist medium. In nature, the plants often grow in living sphagnum moss above a carpet of terrestrial bromeliads. Pot them in pure sphagnum or in fine fir bark with a topdressing of sphagnum. Keep the medium moist but not soggy, as with phalaenopsis.

Vanda
VAN-dah

- ◼ Monopodial
- ◼ Light: High
- ◼ Temperature: Intermediate to warm
- ◼ Flowering: Any season; most species spring to summer
- ◼ Care: Beginner to intermediate

Vandas are some of the most popular cultivated orchids. The broad spectrum of their flower colors includes purple, brown, yellow, white, red, and blue—colors that have been mixed in fantastic combinations and patterns by hybridizers. The flowers are large and long-lived and often appear more than once a year. They are produced from the points where the leaves join the stem.

Vanda plants have an interesting shape; the thick upright stems bear opposite ranks of leaves nourished by a tangle of aerial roots. As with other monopodial orchids, all new growth takes place at the top of the plant. Some species grow very tall—up to 6 feet—but you can keep them at a manageable size by topping them. Most of the hybrids have fairly compact growth habits.

Vanda species are divided into two types, distinguished by the shape of the leaves. Most of the species have straplike leaves, folded into a "V" near the point where the leaf joins the stem. The other group has cylindrical leaves, called terete leaves. Hybridizers have created a third group with semiterete leaves by crossing strap-leaved species with terete-leaved species. Vandas with terete or

Floral stars: Vanda hybrids have glorious flowers for months.

semiterete leaves need intense sun and only flower well outdoors in full sun. Strap-leaved types, however, perform well in bright windows and in greenhouses or lath houses.

Pots and baskets work well for vandas. Coarse bark and tree-fern fiber are the most widely used growing mediums. The fast-growing plants don't like to be crowded, so expect to repot them frequently when they are young. When the plants reach flowering size, repot them only to replace the growing medium when it decays. The plants need

Ascocenda *Chaiyot*, photographed at the Singapore Botanic Garden, shows the strengths of both parents, ascocentrum and vanda.

Vanda *Josephine van Brero* has been used in crosses to give superb "art shades" to the resulting offspring.

Blues and purplish blues are outstanding among the large flowers of vanda hybrids such as this seedling of Bartle Frere × Manila

abundant water and plenty of fertilizer during the growing season, and should not be allowed to dry out completely between waterings. When you water the growing medium, water the aerial roots as well. To avoid splashing water, use a mist bottle to moisten the aerial roots.

SPECIES

■ **VANDA COERULEA:** This famous blue flower is widely grown and extensively hybridized. The symmetrical, rounded petals and sepals are pale blue, netted with veins of deeper blue. The flower sprays are dramatic; five to 15 blossoms are held in each spray, and individual flowers may be up to 4 inches across. The plants reach 4 feet tall, but are easily kept below 2 feet. The strap-shaped leaves are about 10 inches long and 1 inch wide. Many fine cultivars are available, with flower colors ranging from pale to midnight-blue. Native to the highlands of Thailand, Burma, and India, *V. coerulea* needs cool night temperatures. It flowers in the fall and winter.

■ **EUANTHE SANDERIANA (VANDA SANDERIANA):** Although botanists placed this species in a new genus—euanthe—because of its unique lip, most horticultural books and catalogs still list it with the vandas.

Whatever you choose to call it, this is one of the most magnificent of all orchids, producing fragrant, well-shaped flowers from 3 to 4 inches across. The petals and sepals are broad and rounded and open flat. Their color is an exquisite combination of white, yellow, crimson, and brown. The species has many variously colored forms, ranging in hue from purple to red. Four to 10 of the flowers are borne on each inflorescence. The strap-shaped leaves are about 15 inches long. Native to the Philippines, *E. sanderiana* prefers intermediate to warm conditions. It blooms in fall.

HYBRIDS

Because flowers are the focus of hybridization, the blossoms of hybrid vandas are generally superior to those of the species. In many cases the hybrid plants are also more vigorous than the species.

Undoubtedly, the most famous hybrid is *V. Rothschildiana*, a cross of *V. coerulea* and *E. sanderiana*. This hybrid flowers as freely as *V. coerulea*. From this parent, the flowers have picked up their touch of blue and the netted pattern on the sepals and petals. From *E. sanderiana* come a particularly attractive flower shape and an intriguing lip structure. *Vanda* Rothschildiana requires intermediate temperatures.

Vandas have also been crossed with a number of other genera. Some of these intergeneric hybrids are better than the pure vanda hybrids because they require less space and can get by on less light. Smaller hybrids made with vanda and ascocentrum species, known as ascocendas, are especially well-suited to light gardens and other small spaces. The quarter-sized flowers of ascocendas are smaller than those of the vandas, but they make up in color and form what they may lack in size.

Another small hybrid genus suited to growing in windowsills and under light gardens is *Rhynchovanda*, from crossing *Rhynchostylis* × *Vanda*. Seedlings and mericlones of all the intergeneric *Vanda* hybrids are widely available.

TIPS FOR SUCCESS

Vandas offered in bloom at local outlets have probably been grown to the low spike stage in Thailand or Singapore, then flown in and coaxed to the open flower stage in a local greenhouse. Such plants typically arrive in slatted wooden baskets with more of their long, thick roots in evidence than growing medium. At home, place such a basket in a larger one or even a cachepot and lightly pack sphagnum moss all around the roots to help maintain sufficient moisture about them. Daily misting of any exposed roots with water that includes a dilute fertilizer solution (mixed at one-quarter strength) will also help maintain health and prolong the life of the flowers.

Vandas are stressed by repotting, so it's best done only when absolutely necessary, every three or four years, in late winter or early spring. Besides decomposition of the growing medium, another sign that repotting is needed is dying off of the lower part of the plant and loss of leaves from the bottom up. Soak the roots in warm water (86° F) to soften them up, then proceed with repotting.

VANDA CULTIVARS AND HYBRIDS

Vanda Charungrak's Delight
V. coerulea 'Blue Streak'
V. coerulescens 'Bright Eyes'
*V. Dona Rome Sanchez
*V. Fuchs Cheer 'Ontario' HCC/AOS
*V. Fuchs Fuchsia
*V. Fuji Yama
*V. Julia Sorenson
*V. Kasem's Delight
V. luzonica 'York' AM/AOS
*V. Princess Blue
*V. Rari Gold
*V. Sumon Sophonsiri
*V. Surapee Blue
Ascocenda Fuchs Baby Doll 'Redland Spots' AM/AOS
*A. Su-Fun Beauty 'Orange Belle'
*A. Blue Haze

Euanthe sanderiana, *commonly known as* **Vanda sanderiana,** *differs in having a lip with two parts rather than three as in true vandas.*

ORCHID RESOURCES

SOCIETIES:
American Orchid Society
6000 South Olive Avenue
West Palm Beach, FL 33405-4199
561-585-8666 • fax 561-585-0654
www.orchidweb.org
Benefits include the monthly magazine
Orchids, the AOS *Almanac*, a listing of
orchid growers, judges, and local societies
affiliated with the American Orchid
Society, and free access to the AOS
Information Services Department.
e:mail: TheAOS@compuserve.com

PLANTS:
A & P Orchids
110 Peters Rd.
Swansea, MA 02777
508-675-1717 • fax 508-675-0713
www.aandporchids.com

Bloomfield Orchids
251 W. Bloomfield Rd.
Pittsford, NY 14534
716-381-4206
www.frontiernet.net/~bloomfld

Cal-Orchid, Inc.
1251 Orchid Dr.
Santa Barbara, CA 93111
805-967-1312

Carter and Holmes Orchids
629 Mendenhall Rd.
P.O. Box 668
Newberry, SC 29108
803-276-0579
www.carterandholmes.com

Everglades Orchids, Inc.
1101 Tabit Rd.
Belle Glade, FL 33430
561-996-9600 • fax 561-996-7682
www.flinet.com/~evorc

Fender's Flora, Inc.
4315 Plymouth Sorrento Rd.
Apopka, FL 32712
407-886-2464
www.fendersflora.com

Fordyce Orchids
1330 Isabel Ave.
Livermore, CA 94550
925-447-1659

Fox Valley Orchids, Ltd.
1980 Old Willow Rd.
Northbrook, IL 60062
847-205-9660
www.fvo.com

Gemstone Orchids
5750 E. River Rd.
Minneapolis, MN 55432
612-571-3300 • fax 612-571-4209
email: orchidman@isd.net

Hoosier Orchid Co.
8440 West 82nd St.
Indianapolis, IN 46278
317-291-6269
www.hoosierorchid.com

Kensington Orchids
3301 Plyers Mill Rd.
Kensington, MD 20895
301-933-0036 • fax 301-933-9441
www.kensingtonorchids.com

Klehm Growers, Inc.
44 W. 637 State Rt. 72
Hampshire, IL 60140-4766
847-683-4761
www.orchidmall.com/klehm

Miami Orchids
22150 S.W. 147 Ave.
Miami, FL 33170
800-516-5348

Odom's Orchids, Inc.
1611 South Jenkins Rd.
Fort Pierce, FL 34947
561-467-1386
www.odoms.com

Olympia Orchids
27A Windsong Ln.
Friendswood, TX 77546
281-992-1817

Orchids by Hausermann, Inc.
2N134 Addison Rd.
Villa Park, IL 60181-1101
630-543-6855 • fax 630-543-9842
email: hausermann@compuserve.com

Orchids Limited
4630 N. Fernbrook Ln.
Plymouth, MN 55446
612-559-6425 • 800-669-6006
www.orchidweb.com

Parkside Orchid Nursery, Inc.
2503 Mountainview Dr. (Rt. 563)
Ottsville, PA 18942
610-847-8039
www.parksideorchids.com

R.F. Orchids, Inc.
28100 S.W. 182nd Ave.
Homestead, FL 33030
305-245-4570
www.rforchids.com

Rod McLellan Co.
914 S. Claremont St.
San Mateo, CA 94402-1834
800-467-2443
www.rodmclellan.com

Stewart Orchids
3376 Foothill Rd.
Carpinteria, CA 93013
800-621-2450
www.stewartorchids.com

Taylor Orchid Greenhouses
3022 Bluebush Rd.
Monroe, MI 48162
734-243-0180 • fax 734-243-2255

SUPPLIES:
Charley's Greenhouse Supply
17979 State Route 536
Mt. Vernon, WA 98273
800-322-4707 • fax 800-233-3078
www.charleysgreenhouse.com

Environmental Concepts
710 N.W. 57th St.
Ft. Lauderdale, FL 33309
800-327-4635

Full Spectrum Lighting
27 Clover Ln.
Burlington, VT 05401
802-863-3100 • 800-261-3101

Garden Indoors
4538 Indianola Ave.
Columbus, OH 43214
614-262-1600 • 800-833-6868
www.hydrofarm.com

Indoor Garden Supplies
P.O. Box 527-OB
Dexter, MI 48130
734-426-9080
www.indoorgardensupplies.com

Kelley's Korner
P.O. Box 6
Kittery, ME 03904-0006
207-439-0922

OFE International, Inc.
P.O. Box 161081
Miami, FL 33116
305-253-7080 • fax 305-251-8245

Tropical Plant Products, Inc.
P.O. Box 547754
1715 Silver Star Rd.
Orlando, FL 32804-3443
407-293-2451

INDEX

Page numbers in italics denote photographs. Numbers in boldface indicate "Orchid Gallery" entries.

METRIC CONVERSIONS

U.S. Units to Metric Equivalents			Metric Units to U.S. Equivalents		
To Convert From	**Multiply By**	**To Get**	**To Convert From**	**Multiply By**	**To Get**
Inches	25.4	Millimeters	Millimeters	0.0394	Inches
Inches	2.54	Centimeters	Centimeters	0.3937	Inches
Feet	30.48	Centimeters	Centimeters	0.0328	Feet
Feet	0.3048	Meters	Meters	3.2808	Feet
Yards	0.9144	Meters	Meters	1.0936	Yards
Square inches	6.4516	Square centimeters	Square centimeters	0.1550	Square inches
Square feet	0.0929	Square meters	Square meters	10.764	Square feet
Square yards	0.8361	Square meters	Square meters	1.1960	Square yards
Acres	0.4047	Hectares	Hectares	2.4711	Acres
Cubic inches	16.387	Cubic centimeters	Cubic centimeters	0.0610	Cubic inches
Cubic feet	0.0283	Cubic meters	Cubic meters	35.315	Cubic feet
Cubic feet	28.316	Liters	Liters	0.0353	Cubic feet
Cubic yards	0.7646	Cubic meters	Cubic meters	1.308	Cubic yards
Cubic yards	764.55	Liters	Liters	0.0013	Cubic yards

To convert from degrees Fahrenheit (F) to degrees Celsius (C), first subtract 32, then multiply by $\frac{5}{9}$.

To convert from degrees Celsius to degrees Fahrenheit, multiply by $\frac{9}{5}$, then add 32.